AF651316

Concept Publishing Co.
Rs 300/-

RECLAIMING WASTELANDS

RECLAIMING WASTELANDS

A Case Study of Amethi Block
District Sultanpur

H.R. YADAV

CONCEPT PUBLISHING COMPANY,
NEW DELHI-110059

ISBN 81-7022-273-7

First Published 1990

© Hridai Ram Yadav 1989

Hridai Ram Yadav (*b*. 1957)

Published by

Ashok Kumar Mittal
Concept Publishing Company
A/15-16, Commercial Block, Mohan Garden
NEW DELHI-110059

Printed in India by

Deep Printers
NEW DELHI-110015

Contents

List of Maps

List of Tables

Acknowledgements

I express my sincere gratitude to Prof. L.S. Bhat and Prof. A. Kundu for their inspiration, suggestions and comments.

I acknowledge the financial support given by the Indian Council of Social Science Research for the work reported in this volume. My heartiest thanks are due to Shri D.P. Yadav, M.P., Chairman, NIWARD, for constant encouragement and inspiration. Thanks are also due to Shri Rudal Yadav and Shri S.K. Singh for their constant help in collection of informations at village level and to Shri Samarpal Singh for the cartographic work. I am thankful to Shri Anil Yadav for typing the manuscript.

I record my gratefulness to all the officials of the National Institute of Wastelands and Rural Development for their constant help.

H.R. YADAV

1

Introduction

1.1 Statement of the Problem

Population growth in India and the growing demand for goods and services have imposed severe constraints on the natural resources, especially on the forest and green cover. This phenomenon continues to affect the quality of life of the rural masses who constitute 75% of the Indian population. Increased exploitation of natural resources for meeting the growing demands of the ever-increasing population and industry for food, fibre, fishery products, fodder, fruit, fuelwood and other materials has led to environmental degradation and rapid expansion of wastelands. At present, India has as much as 175 million ha degraded land out of the total area of only 328 million ha. Satellite imagery indicates that we are losing about 1.3 million ha forest per year. In his broadcast to the nation on 5 January 1985, Prime Minister, Shri Rajiv Gandhi, observed "continuing deforestation has brought us face to face with a major ecological and socio-economic crisis. The trend must be halted. I propose immediately to set up a National Wastelands Development Board with the object of bringing 5 million ha of land every year under fuelwood and fodder plantations. We shall develop a people's movement for afforestation."

The nation's present firewood requirement is more than 130 million tonnes per year, of which only 39 million tonnes are fetched from the forest. The life of the adivasis and scheduled castes is interwoven with the forest and unless there is replenishment through positive afforestation, there will be total breakdown of their socio-economic system.

Growing industrialization and use of chemicals and pesticides have had serious negative impacts on the life of the Indian people. In the historic words of Shrimati Indira Gandhi "In his arrogance with his increasing knowledge and ability, man has ignored his dependence on the earth and has lost communion with it. He no longer puts his ear to the ground so that the earth can whisper its secret to him. The national song which inspired our freedom movement describes our land as one endowed with water and fruit, rich with the greenness of growing plants. We must make this true not only of India but of all lands".

Thus, as a poverty alleviation programme for the rural poor and weaker sections, a positive programme towards providing forests, fodder and green cover as well as for growing raw materials so as to cater to the needs of industries and to open up new employment avenues should be taken up. The need to develop wastelands is thus paramount.

The massive action envisaged will mean having a fresh look at policies and priorities, formulation of new and innovative strategies, new and more appropriate structures, fresh initiatives that will make afforestation a movement of everyone's concern and ultimately ushering in a revolution to green the wastelands.

The magnitude of the problem and the gravity of the situation are evident from the following facts :

(i) In agriculture sector, out of 143 m ha area, 40-60 million ha is considered degraded.

(ii) In the forestry sector, out of 75 million ha area, 40 million ha is degraded, 30 million ha is without tree cover and 5 million ha is with only shrubs.

(iii) The pasture and grazing lands and other public lands are the most degraded ones, because they have also been the most neglected areas. We are losing about 6000 million tonnes of soil equivalent to 5.37-8.4 million tonnes nutrients per annum, which represents a production loss of 30-40 million tonnes of foodgrains per year.

(iv) About 40 million ha area is flood prone and

260 million ha is drought prone. Besides soil erosion by water and wind, there are several other causes of soil degradation.

By 2000 AD, the population of India (1000 million) will require 225 m tonnes foodgrains, 30 m tonnes sugar, 695 m kg tea, 159 m kg coffee, 10.2 m tonnes vegetable oils, 17 m bales cotton, and 70.0 m m^3 wood. For this, 40 m ha area will have to be brought under food production, for fuel and other needs and 10 m ha each for the production of crops and fodder along with 6 m ha for increased urbanization. The estimated fuel requirement is 230 m m^3.

The above observations point to the urgency of (a) launching and strengthening educational programmes on wasteland development and afforestation by and for the farmers and government officials as well as the general public so that the minimum needs of the poor people, scheduled castes and scheduled tribes are met ; (b) a massive campaign for increasing the area under productive use, i.e. production of fuel and fodder and materials for rural and cottage industries ; (c) development of appropriate technologies for different climatic, soil and topographic conditions for wasteland utilization ; and (d) identification of optimum patches of land in different locations with respect to water and soil resources for maximization of benefits.

1.2 Literature Survey

Detailed literature survey has revealed that scanty information is available on themes directly related to the development of wastelands and their reclamation. A few relevant studies are mentioned below.

Gedroiz[1] has discussed the distribution and reclamation of saline lands, with particular reference to reclamation measures and economics of reclamation. Sharma[2] has made an effort to analyse ravine lands and their distribution, with special reference to the Chambal Valley. His discussion is based on geomorphic evaluation. He has explained rejuvenation as an important parameter for ravine formation. He has also suggested several measures for the reclamation of ravine lands. Singh[3] has discussed agricultural land reclamation, with particular reference to selected villages of Koil Tehsil of Aligarh District in UP. Singh's work constitutes a new approach to wasteland studies. She did an exhaustive survey of land, classified as other uncultivated land, excluding fallows and fallows other than current fallows, to locate the areas where large blocks of land are available for reclamation and resettlement. Maps for all villages were collected from the tehsil headquarters at Aligarh. The general aspects, including the relief, drainage, climate and soil of the area were studied in detail. Suitable measures for reclamation, according to the conditions in different areas, estimates of the cost of reclamation and colonization, financial assistance and agricultural extension and necessary training for the settlers, were suggested. Some of the prominent usar blocks were also studied. Finally, estimations were made of the economic aspects of such reclamation in terms of the expenditure involved, likely addition to foodgrain production, employment and the income that would accrue to the settlers.

Yadav[4] has classified the wastelands of Sultanpur district into various types, viz., waterlogged, usar, banjar, old fallow, fallow kankrili, ravine, etc. He has explained the distribution of wastelands in the district at village, block and tehsil levels for the years 1977-78 and 1981-82. The increase in area of wastelands during these years was also studied. Various environmental and anthropogenic factors responsible for the formation of such wastelands were explained with the help of correlation matrix and stepwise regression analysis. Genesis and capability classification of the wastelands were explained. Yadav[4] has also discussed reclamation strategies for various wasteland types as practised in 1 ha of wasteland in selected villages. The economics of reclamation has been discussed, various planning methods described and suggestions put forth. Yadav has suggested that reclamation of wastelands should be started as a strategy to increase the net sown area under agricultural production as a means of improving the socio-economic condition of the rural poor masses.

Dhir[5] has identified and defined wastelands on the basis

of revenue records. He has made a survey of the wastelands and attempted their classification on land use basis too. Sarkar[6] studied the vegetation of semi-arid wastelands. He has discussed various dependable indicators for assessing the extent of degradation of such lands.

Sen[7] attempted to analyse the types and extent of wastelands in Western Rajasthan. He studied the typology of wastelands on the basis of land utilization survey conducted using remote sensing technique, topographical technique and aerial photography. He has classified wastelands as sandy, saline waste, storms waste, gravelly waste, rocky waste, rocks, sandy waste with open shrubs and rocks and gravelly waste with open shrubs. He also attempted to map various wasteland types in Western Rajasthan.

Saxena[8] studied multi-purpose plants which can survive in wastelands. He has discussed the soil conservation characteristics and animal husbandry practices and economic contributions of multipurpose trees and shrubs for wasteland development. Chopra[9] has discussed the economic importance of various horticultural plants which are suitable for planting under arid conditions and can be easily adopted by the farmers, enabling them to make good profits.

Shankarnarayan[10] has dealt with rehabilitation of wastelands. According to him, such lands can be easily identified and used for agroforestry purposes. He has concluded that agroforestry developed on the wastelands is the key to the rehabilitation of wastelands. Mittal[11] has explained the role of livestock farming in wasteland development. He has explained various livestock farming methods in wastelands where crop production is impracticable.

Dhir[12] has analysed the recent awareness programmes related to ecological crisis and fuelwood and fodder shortage. Environmental degradation has caused serious problems for the rural poor masses in respect of fuelwood and fodder. He has also reviewed the work of various organizations at national and state levels involved in developmental activities in this area. Verma[13] analysed the principles and practices behind gully erosion and the different approaches to gully reclamation.

Chinnamani[11] has discussed the roles of forestry, social forestry and agroforestry in ravine reclamation. He has described the concept of ravine land and its distribution in India. According to him, through ravine reclamation, the minimum fuel requirements of the rural poor can be easily met.

Singh[15] studied the distribution of wastelands in India on the basis of rainfall. He has discussed various inputs needed for the development of dry land agriculture. He has also dealt with reclamation of wastelands for farming, water storage in the form of ponds and tanks, improved agriculture, social forestry and agroforestry, including horticultural activities. According to him, wasteland development work should be linked with dryland agricultural activities.

Bhumbla[16], while dealing with the reclamation of alkali soils in UP, has highlighted the essential components of wasteland development technology which are important for the reclamation of alkali soils. Pant[17] has discussed the problem of reclamation of usar lands, in particular the importance of proper planning in this respect. He has emphasized the role of NABARD in the drives towards reclamation of usar lands. Aggarwal[18] also made an exhaustive study of usar lands in UP and their reclamation for agricultural and forestry purposes.

Khanduri[19] has discussed the role of climate and topography in the formation of usar lands and has emphasized the need to reclaim usar lands on a large scale for agricultural and agroforestry purposes.

Shrivastava[20] has explained the role of Prosopis in wasteland development. According to him, Prosopis can be easily grown in soil having pH above 9. According to him, keeping in view the extent of usar and other types of wasteland, there is considerable scope for planting such species in these areas. Besides being a good source of firewood, Prosopis gives high quality charcoal.

Studies conducted in various developing countries have shown that more than 1.5 million people meet their energy requirements in the form of wood and charcoal. Hegde[21] has also discussed wasteland development through plantation of

Prosopis. According to him, plantation of Prosopis in wastelands will not only enable conservation and reclamation of the land, but also provide large quantities of biomass, making it an economically viable proposition.

Sharma[22] has suggested integration of agroforestry with goat husbandry in wastelands. He has proposed a three-tier agroforestry scheme for reclaiming wastelands with people's participation, particularly of women, tribals and children. He claims that his scheme can help to bring rapid improvement in the soil status and fertility, thereby enabling regeneration of productive phytomass in fragile ecozones. It has the potential to benefit the below-poverty line population through production of fuel, fodder and fruits.

Tolba[23] has attributed farmland degradation to over-cultivation, unskilled irrigation and overgrazing. He has also suggested various measures to check such land degradation, whereby livestock productivity can be increased without damaging the environment. He has also discussed the role of industrial pollution in the creation of wastelands.

Bhumla and Khare[24] have discussed the ways in which wastelands are formed through water erosion, soil erosion, floods, waterlogging, soil salinity, soil alkalinisation, etc. They have also suggested measures for reclaiming various categories of wastelands.

Sen[35] made use of photo–interpretation technique to map and estimate the wastelands of the arid zone of Rajasthan. Shankarnarayan *et al.*[26] tried this using the remote sensing technique. They have also suggested several land utilization steps for arid zones. Banerjee[27] has dealt with the reclamation of wasteland in laterite tracts of Eastern India.

Abrol and Joshi have[28] discussed the economic viability of reclamation of alkali land, with special reference to agriculture and forestry. He has also discussed the various technologies developed for afforestation along with their cost-benefit analysis. The economics of agroforestry for wasteland reclamation has been discussed by Mathur[29]. Shah[30] has attempted to analyse the economics of wasteland development under the projects undertaken by Gujarat State Rural Development Corporation. He has also discussed various techniques being used to reclaim wastelands, as also their cost-benefit analysis. Venkataraman[31] has discussed the designing, planning and financing of tree plantation projects for wastelands. Chowdhary[32] has discussed various strategies for forestry development in wastelands, with particular reference to the policy aspects and the achievements made so far.

It is obvious from the above literature survey that most of the studies are concentrated mainly on the problems relating to reclamation of saline and alkaline soils. Very few studies have been conducted on spatial distribution of wastelands. There have also been attempts to study the possible reclamation measures along with the economics of reclamation. In general, the main thrust has been on the pedogenic factors while probing into the causes of wastelands formation. The earlier studies have failed to provide satisfactory explanations for the growth of wastelands, the thrust having been limited only to a few determinants. The problems have not been examined in totality in the sense that the studies were restricted to the extent of the chosen problem. Though a variety of measures for the reclamation of wastelands have been suggested, adequate attention has not been paid to their adaptability to particular land types.

Keeping the above facts in view, an entirely different approach to the problem has been attempted in the present study. The focus is primarily on the following aspects :

—Identifying the problem of wastelands at village level in specific contexts. Such analysis at micro-level would help in analysing the relative merits and demerits of various wasteland reclamation measures.

—Assessing the prominent features of various types of wastelands.

—Analysing the factors responsible for wasteland formation at the village level.

—Assessing the relative merits of various reclamation practices as used in the field for the reclamation of wasteland for social forestry, agroforestry and agriculture.

—Estimating the economics of wasteland reclamation in practical terms for social forestry, agroforestry and agriculture.

—Suggesting suitable strategies for the reclamation of wastelands according to their physical suitability.

1.3 Objectives of the Study

The following were the main objectives of the present study :

(1) To study the distribution of wastelands at village level in Amethi Block of Sultanpur District, UP.

(2) To analyse the growth of wastelands in Sultanpur District and Amethi Block for the periods 1977-78 to 1981-82 and 1981-82 to 1986-87.

(3) To identify the environmental and anthropogenic factors responsible for the formation of wastelands of various types.

(4) To explain various correlates of wastelands at village level.

(5) To suggest suitable practical remedies for the reclamation of various wastelands, keeping in view their suitability for developing social forestry, agroforestry and agriculture.

(6) To analyse the economics of wasteland reclamation through input-output analysis.

1.4 Choice of Indicators

The indicators selected for the present study fall under two categories : dependent and independent variables. The choice of independent variables from among a large number of parameters involved needs careful consideration in the sense that they must in one way or the other be associated with the selected dependent variables. These variables can be of various types representing both environmental and anthropogenic aspects.

(*a*) *Dependent variables* (wastelands)

(i) Waterlogged land
(ii) Usar land
(iii) Banjar land
(iv) Old fallow land

(v) Fallow land
(vi) Other types of wasteland.

(*b*) *Independent variables*

I. Environmental factors
   (a) Slope
   (b) Ruggedness number
   (c) Drainage density
   (d) Quality of water (pH)
   (e) Behaviour of water table
   (f) NPK status of the soil
   (g) pH value of the soil.

II. Anthropogenic factor
   Land concentration (Gini's coefficient)

1.5 Hypothesis

Various environmental and anthropogenic parameters (independent variables) show varying trends of interrelationship with the type of wasteland (dependent variables).

—It is assumed that waterlogged land may have a positive correlation with slope, ruggedness number and drainage density, and it may have negative correlation with the quality of water (pH), behaviour of water table and pH value of the soil.

—Usar land may have a positive correlation with quality of water (pH), pH value of the soil and NPK status of the soil, and negative correlation with slope, ruggedness number, drainage density and behaviour of the water table.

—Banjar land may have positive correlation with slope, ruggedness number, drainage density, quality of water (pH), behaviour of the water table, NPK status and pH value of the soil.

—Old fallow land may have positive correlation with slope, ruggedness number, drainage density, quality of water (pH), behaviour of the water table, pH value of the soil, NPK status of the soil and land concentration.

—It is assumed that fallow land may have a positive relationship with slope, ruggedness number, drainage density, quality of water (pH), behaviour of the water table, NPK status of the soil, pH value of the soil and land concentration.

—It is assumed that other types of wastelands may have a positive correlation with slope, ruggedness number, drainage density, behaviour of the water table, pH value of the soil, land concentration and negative correlation with the quality of water (pH) and NPK status of the soil.

—It is assumed that wastelands are the result of complex interaction of processes which can be designated as compound processes.

—If the stage of wastelands development is intense, the cost of their reclamation will be high.

1.6 Database

Since the study is based on micro-level information, i.e., village level information on the wastelands, due attention has been paid to its collection to achieve a dependable database, which can be used for propounding a theory. Databases vary from one theme to another according to the nature of the problem. The database for the present study is made up of the following components :

I. *Records*

Land revenue records at Muhafijikhana of Amethi Tehsil. All the revenue officials starting from Lakhpal. Kanoongo, Registrar Kanoongo, Naib Tehsildar and Tehsildar of the Tehsil were approached through personal communications.

II. *Statistical books of Sultanpur District for 1981-82 and 1986-87*

III. *Field Work*

Most of the data have been collected through field work involving questionnaires, interviewing of revenue officials and villagers, including village heads and personal field observations.

IV. *Survey of India Topo-Sheets*

63F/10, 11, 12, 14, 15, 16

63J/3, 4, 7, 8, 11, 12 63K/5, 9.

V. *Personal Communications Addressed to*

1. Office of the District Magistrate, Sub-divisional Magistrate, Office of the Dy Director, Soil Conservation, Sharda Sahayak Command, Amethi, Sultanpur.
2. Dy Director. Agriculture, Sultanpur
3. Office of the Executive Engineer, Sharda Sahayak Khand 16 and 49, Sultanpur.
4. Office of the Executive Engineer, Tubewell, Sultanpur.
5. Office of the Director, Social Forestry, Sultanpur.

1.7 (a) Quantitative Methods

(i) *Wastelands*

The selected blocks have wastelands which are water-logged, usar, banjar, old fallow and fallow, while in Sultanpur District there are two more categories of wastelands, viz., kankarili and ravine. From the revenue officials data for only usar banjar, old fallow and fallow types of wastelands were available: for the waterlogged and other wasteland categories no data were available. Therefore, for these categories, data were collected personally and by interviewing revenue officials, villagers, village heads, etc. during field work in the villages of Amethi Block. In this way, information on wastelands was collected at village, block and tehsil levels for the years 1977-78, 1981-82 and 1986-87. The extent of each waste-land as percentage of the total area was calculated.

(ii) *Slope*

Topo-sheets of the Survey of India were consulted to find out the heights of various villages. The available spot height as well as contour value were considered and plotted on the village map. According to the local elevation, some additional spots were plotted on the same map and then contour lines were drawn; the minimum and maximum contour lines were then identified. The average number of contour crossings per mile was computed. The average slope was calculated using Wentworth formula:

$$\text{Av. slope} = \frac{\text{Av. No. of contour crossings/mile} \times \text{contour interval}}{3361 \text{ (constant)}}.$$

The computed values of slope were cross-checked with the values available with the Office of the Executive Engineer (Irrigation), Sharda Sahayak Khand.

(iii) *Ruggedness number*

Based on field observations, drainage lines were drawn on the actual map of the village and their total length was divided by the area to calculate the drainage density of the village. The value of relative relief was computed by subtracting the minimum height from the maximum height of the village. The ruggedness number was calculated as follows :

$$\text{Ruggedness No.} = \frac{\text{Drainage density} \times \text{Relative relief}}{5280}.$$

(iv) *Drainage density*

The natural and artificial drainage lines were drawn for the selected village and the length of drainage lines per unit area was measured. The drainage density was computed as follows :

$$\text{Drainage density} = \frac{\text{Total drainage length}}{\text{Total area}}.$$

(v) *Quality of water (pH)*

The data on quality of water (pH) were collected from the Office of the Executive Engineer, UP Jal Nigam, Tubewell Irrigation Department.

(vi) *Behaviour of water table*

Information on the behaviour of water table was collected from the Office of the Executive Engineer (Tubewell), UP

Jal Nigam, and Ground Water Survey Division of the District. The data were supplemented with personal field observations of the wells during the field work. The depths were tape-measured and the data generalized at village level.

(vii) *NPK & pH value of the soil*

Data on nitrogen, phosphate and potash concentrations and pH values of the soil were collected from the District Laboratory, Sultanpur. A few soil samples were also got tested at the soil laboratory.

(viii) *Land concentration*

Land concentration was computed using Gini's coefficient, which enables the value of inequality of the land (area) to be estimated.

(ix) *Choice of samples*

To identify the factors influencing various wasteland types, all the villages of Amethi Block were covered. The basic objective was to work out practical remedies for the reclamation of wastelands as well as the economics of reclamation for developing social forestry, agroforestry and agriculture.

Three villages were selected on the basis of stratified sampling. A village with usar land having high pH value of soil was selected for social forestry. For agroforestry, a village with usar land with low pH value of soil was selected and a village with banjar land was chosen for agricultural development.

(x) *Explanatory system*

Study of causal relationships among dependent variables (waterlogged land, usar land, banjar land, old fallow land, fallow land. kankrili land. ravine land and other types of wastelands) and independent variables (environmental, morphometric, hydrologic, pedogenic and anthropogenic factors) is an essential concern of any scientific investigation. Precise quantitative measurements of the degree and direction of correlation were made as per Karl Pearson's coefficient of correlation. The correlation matrix was prepared to work out the correlations of independent variables for various types of wastelands.

Stepwise regression analysis was done as the final step.

(xi) *Cartographic techniques*

Various cartographic methods were adopted to represent and depict the data in graphic form.

Choroplething was used to show the distribution of wastelands at village level.

1.8 Choice of the Study Area

The choice of the area for an analysis of this type involving a micro-level situation is very important. In the present study, Amethi Block in Sultanpur District was selected because of the wide variation in wasteland types from one village to another. Wastelands cover 13.72% of the area of the district and there is wide variation in wasteland types at all three levels, i.e., tehsil, block and village. The growth of each type of wasteland at tehsil and block levels was observed to be significant. Fortunately, the area has potential for agricultural development through reclamation of wastelands for the economic betterment of the district as a whole.

1.9 Choice of the Time Period

The choice of time period is very much a matter of convenience, as the analysis is based on field observations. For field work, 1981-82 and 1986-87 were taken as the base years. For observing the temporal variation, five years' gap was decided upon. Thus, changes in wasteland extension were noted over the periods 1977-78 to 1981-82 and 1981-82 to 1986-87.

1.10 Geographic Background of the Study Area

Amethi Block of Sultanpur District is located in Faizabad Division of Eastern UP. The district is situated between the parallels of 25° 59′ and 26° 46′ north and 81° 32′ and 82° 41′

east. According to the Surveyor General of India, the area of the district is 4425 sq km. while the total area of Amethi block is 4052 acres Geographically, Sultanpur District lies in the eastern region of the state. The district is bounded in the east by Jaunpur and Azamgarh Districts, in the west by Rai Bareilly and Barabanki Districts, in the north by Faizabad District and in the south by Pratapgarh District. It comprises 5 tehsils—Sadar Sultanpur (6 blocks), Kadipur (5 blocks), Amethi (4 blocks), Gauriganj (3 blocks) and Musaffirkhana (4 blocks).

There are 22 blocks (Map 1) in Sultanpur District and it comprises 2535 villages. The headquarter of all the tehsils is Sultanpur City, situated on the right bank of river Gomati. Amethi Block of Amethi Tehsil is situated in the north west corner of Sultanpur District. There are 85 villages in Amethi block.

The administrative set-up in Amethi Block (village-wise) is shown in Map 2.

1.10.1 History of the Area

Traditionally, it is known that a town was founded on the left bank of river Gomati by Kusa, son of Rama and was called Kushbhavanpur. At the time of the Muslim conquest, the district was held by the Bhars, etc. situated within District and no reference to it can be found in the Persian history. Local tradition asserts that Kushbhavanpur was conquered by Ala-ud-din, but probably there has been a mistake about the name of the conqueror. The district formed part of Jaunpur Kingdom in the 15th century and after the downfall of Lodi dynasty it was incorporated in Delhi empire. After the redistribution made by Akbar, the present area fell partly in the Subah of Oudh and partly in that of Allahabad, but 250 years later, the whole district came under the Nawab of Oudh. In 1856, when Oudh was annexed, a district was formed which included portions of what are now Barabanki and Rai Bareilly Districts, while additions were made to it from Faizabad. The district was named Sultanpur and assumed its present shape in 1869[33].

Many ancient mounds found in the district are connected

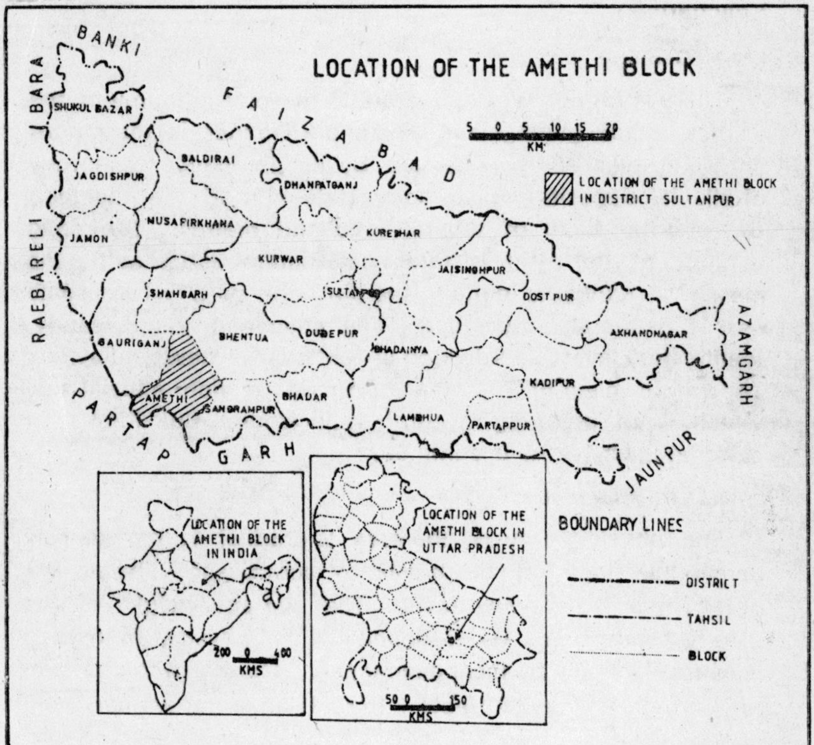
LOCATION OF THE AMETHI BLOCK
5 0 5 10 15 20
KM.
LOCATION OF THE AMETHI BLOCK
IN DISTRICT SULTANPUR
BANKI
BARA
FAIZABAD
RAEBARELI
AZAMGARH
JAUNPUR
PARTAPGARH
SHUKUL BAZAR
BALDIRAI
JAGDISHPUR
DHANPATGANJ
JAMON
MUSAFIRKHANA
KUREBHAR
KURWAR
JAISINGHPUR
SHAHGARH
SULTANPUR
DOST PUR
GAURIGANJ
BHENTUA
DUBEPUR
BHADAINYA
AKHANDNAGAR
KADIPUR
AMETHI
BHADAR
SANGRAMPUR
LAMBHUA
PARTAPPUR
LOCATION OF THE
AMETHI BLOCK
IN INDIA
200 0 400
KMS
LOCATION OF THE
AMETHI BLOCK IN
UTTAR PRADESH
50 0 150
KMS
BOUNDARY LINES
DISTRICT
TAHSIL
BLOCK

MAP – 1

by local tradition with the Bhars. Some of them have yielded Buddhist relics, but no regular excavations have been done. The main sacred places connected with the Ramayana epic are Sitakund, a bathing ghat on the Gomati close to Sultanpur and Dhopap, lower down the same river. At the latter place are the ruins of a fort built by Sher Shah, which is known as Shahgarh.

1.10.2 Geology

There is no noteworthy feature in the physiognomy of the district. Thus, geologically, Sultanpur District is not important. The plain is characterized by an unrelieved monotony of alluvial deposits which completely shroud the old land surface to a depth of several thousand metres. The solid geology of the plain is totally obscured underneath the mantle[34]. Kankar is found in the northern part, where some usar lands are also observed. The solids are mainly sandy, loamy and clayey, sub-divided into Khadar or newer alluvium. The whole plain of the area is formed of rich alluvial soil which is of great agricultural importance. But Kankar or calcareous limestone is common.

1.10.3 Physiography

The physiography of the area is gradual with a scarcely perceptible slope from north-west to south-east. The surface of the area is generally level. The average height of the area is 110 metres. Heterogeneity of the physical landscape is caused actually by local eminences. These are the perceptible notches of banjar tracts. In real sense, the scenery is of varied character.

The Ganga-Yamuna Doab is part of the Indo-Gangetic Plain. This plain is a depression between the Himalaya in the north and the Deccan Plateau in the south. It has been filled by the alluvium brought down by the Himalayan rivers. The composition of this alluvium commenced after the final upheaval of the mountain and has continued all through the Pliestocene up to the present[35]. Various hypotheses have been put forward to explain the geological evolution of this plain.

The depth of the alluvium is not known accurately. Boring

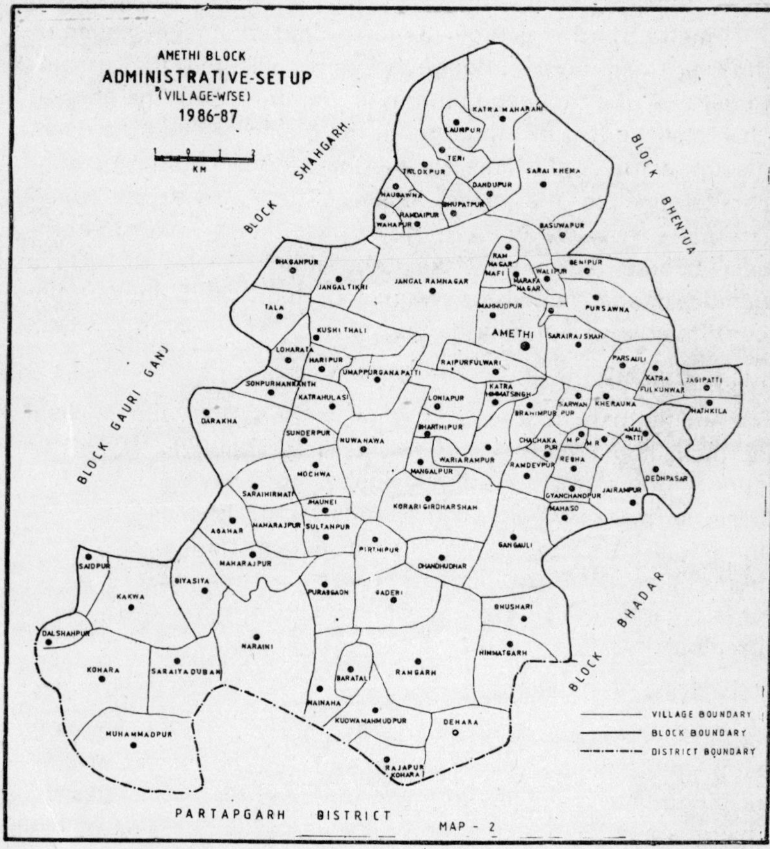
AMETHI BLOCK
ADMINISTRATIVE-SETUP
(VILLAGE-WISE)
1986-87
KM
BLOCK SHAHGARH
BLOCK BHENTUA
BLOCK GAURI GANJ
BLOCK BHADAR
PARTAPGARH DISTRICT
VILLAGE BOUNDARY
BLOCK BOUNDARY
DISTRICT BOUNDARY
KATRA MAHARANI
SARAI KHEMA
DANDUPUR
BASUWAPUR
BENIPUR
PURSAWNA
JANGAL RAMNAGAR
JANGAL TIKRI
BHAGANPUR
TALA
KUSHI THALI
LOHARATA
HARIPUR
AMETHI
MAHMUDPUR
RAIPURFULWARI
PARSAULI
JAGIPATTI
HATHKILA
KHERAUNA
DARAKHA
SUNDERPUR
HUWANAWA
MOCHWA
MANGALPUR
WARIARAMPUR
RAMDEVPUR
RESHA
GYANCHANDPUR
JAIRAMPUR
DEDHPASAR
MAHASO
SULTANPUR
KORARI GIRDHARSHAH
AGAHAR
MAHARAJPUR
PIRTHIPUR
DHANDHUDHAR
GANGAULI
SAIDPUR
KAKWA
BIYASIYA
PURASGAON
GADERI
BHUSHARI
HIMMATGARH
DALSHAHPUR
NARAINI
KOHARA
SARAIYA DUBAN
RAMGARH
BARATALI
MAINAHA
KUOWA MAHMUDPUR
DEHARA
MUHAMMADPUR
RAJAPUR KOHARA

MAP - 2

down mainly for artesian wells has penetrated only up to 1.606 metres in the recent alluvium strata[36]. Geologists differ in their estimates of the thickness of the alluvial deposits. On the basis of observations, Glennie[37] estimated about 1.950 metres.

1.10.4 Drainage

Amethi Block is part of the integrated drainage system of the river Chamroura, although different nalas join the stream. In general, the drainage pattern is dendritic and the general characteristic features throughout the plains are that the rivers meet at acute angles and several nalas form parallel or sub-parallel lines to the main stream. There are several small streams. River Chamroura flows from north-west to south-east, There are tanks, lakes and jhils. There are also a number of shallow jhils or swamps, but none of them is of any considerable size or importance.

1.10.5 Climate

Amethi experiences a rhythm of seasons with reversal of prevailing winds. The reversal is regularly felt twice during the year. From November to May, winds blow from the west and are of the continental character, whereas from June to October, they are of oceanic origin and come from the east. This complete reversal of direction of winds on a gigantic scale between summer and winter is responsible for monsoons.

1.10.5(a) *Temperature*

The monsoon currents are the outcome of changes in temperature which tend to set up surface pressure differences, resulting in a low pressure over the land and high pressure over the adjoining areas and vice versa. Hottest months of the year are May and June. The mean temperatures during these months are 32.3 and 31.7°C respectively. The extreme maximum in the month of June is 45.0°C. This is due to the sun's rays falling almost vertically. Conversely, the extreme minimum occurring in the month of December is 4.4°C, since the sun is low during this month owing to the earth's position in winter solstice.

1.10.5(b) *Pressure and Winds*

The pressure is 985 millibars during the months of June, July and August. In the month of December, it rises to 1,004 millibars. A shallow cell of high pressure with seaward gradient develops over the land in December and January, In summer, tbe pressure gradient is towards the land. The shallow depressions visiting the district in a cyclonic form ascend from the Bay of Bengal. But the high pressure cells in December and January reach here from west causing rough weather and little rain.

1.10.5(c) *Moisture and Humidity*

The principal factor which determines the potentiality of rainfall is the humidity level in the atmosphere. Humidity is high in the months of June, July, August and September. The temperature, during these months, is also high and the pressure is subsequently low. The winds are dry during the months of March, April and May and the relative humidity is comparatively low.

1.10.5(d) *Rainfall*

Ninety per cent of the annual rainfall is received within a short period of four months, i.e. from mid-October to June. Rainfall during the other months is scanty and sporadic. The annual normal rainfall for the area is 1,000 milimetres, but it is unevenly distributed over the year.

(i) *Annual variability of rainfall* : Due to the high annual variability of rainfall, the prosperity of the farmers depends largely on the uniform distribution of annual rainfall. An annual variability of 12% or more makes an area susceptible to famine[38]. In this respect, Amethi stands very often in the danger of super-abundance or deficiency of rainfall. There are some places which experience drought conditions, while many others are liable to face serious flood and waterlogging conditions due to heavy rain during the same year.

(ii) *Seasonal and monthly variability of rainfall* : Seasonal and monthly variability of rainfall is rather more significant than the annual variability from the point of view of agricultural operations. If the rainfall in the month of June is insignificant or excessive, it can delay the sowing of the early Kharif crops and thus reduce the returns. If the rainfall is heavy and alternates with long intervals, floods and droughts are experienced simultaneously. The state of abnormality frequently causes havoc and the whole cropping pattern is affected seriously. Early or late retreat of the summer in September and October affects maturing of the Kharif crops. On the other hand, heavy rainfall may cause postponement or restriction of sowing of Rabi crops[39].

Thus, taking all the weather elements together and considering the variations in their incidence, the year is divided into three distinct seasons :

(1) The season of rain—mid-June to October.
(2) The cold weather season—November to February
(3) The hot weather season—March to mid-June.

Thus, we find that the climate of the area is mild and healthy. West winds prevail from October to June, gradually increasing in strength as the hot season approaches. The northern part of the district receives more rainfall than the southern part.

1.10.6 Soils

Soils of the area are transported from the sedimentary rock of the Himalayas and the products of the decomposition of these rocks have been deposited over this tract through water action. Therefore, the soils of the district fall under the alluvial group of the Indo-Gangetic Plain. Scientific data regarding the soils of the district are not available. A brief account of the soils and land classification based on the texture of the soils is, however, prepared by the revenue authorities to assess the land revenue. The main factors governing the system of classification are texture, colour, availability of water and the level of the land[40]. On the basis of texture, the soils of the district have been sub-divided into the following groups :

(*i*) *Bangar Soil*

Bangar (upland plain) soils vary from sandy loam to stiff clay, depending upon topography and drainage. Bangar lands arise on the basis of the principle that when a river grows older, its deposits subsequently occupy a lower position along its basin and the terraces and the flood plain are gradually left free by the spreading action of water during the old age of the river. These raised uplands, which are called bangar, are again eroded by the newer channels, but they always ramain above the flood plain and are never affected.

(*ii*) *Loamy Soil*

This soil is locally called "Domat Soil". It is extensively distributed over the bangar or upland plain. Patches of loamy soil are noticeable. The patches of Domat soil are very well drained. Sand and clay are present in this soil in almost equal proportions ; therefore, they can be easily recognized. Depending on the fertility, Domat soil has been further divided into : (1) Domat Avval, (2) Domat Doam, and (3) Domat Soam. Depending upon the percentage of sand, the colour varies from yellow to brown. The sub-soil is brownish and yellow, sometimes mixed together and sometimes with alternating layers. The water holding capacity also varies according to the texture. Loamy soil is preferred by the cultivators, since it can be used for double and multiple cropping.

(*iii*) *Clayey Loam*

Clayey loam soil is locally known as Matiyar soil and has grey or yellowish grey colour at the surface. The sub-soil in the lower horizons is dark grey in colour. In comparison to the Domat soil, the percentage of clay in it is high ; its water retention capacity is also very high. It was recorded at the time of the field study that this type of soil is found almost in every village. Matiyar soil is seen to occupy low level areas, which results in accumulation of rainwater. Consequently, the soil responds well to paddy crop, Sometimes this soil is characterized by the presence of calcareous concretions which are leached from the surface and get accumulated at various depths in the form of Kankar.

(iv) Calayey Soil

This soil is locally known as "Dhankhar Soil" and is grey to dark grey in colour. Dhankhar soil, as its name indicates, is largely used for growing dhan, i.e., paddy. It has compact and cloddy structure and becomes sticky when wet and very hard when dry. It is mostly used for raising a single crop of late paddy ; during other parts of the year it is almost left idle. The villagers call fields with these soils as "Jadhan's Khet" (type of paddy land). In fact, ploughing and sowing are almost impossible when this land is dry. Clayey soil is found only in small patches. It mostly lies in the vicinities of tals and jhils and occasionally near low-lying areas.

(v) Khadar Soil

Khadar soil is mainly confined to the flood plains of rivers and jhils. Khadar soil is generally light, but is rich in calcareous matter. Beds of sand and clay are deposited as alternate layers. The soil in the vicinity of rivers has more sand in comparison to soil lying away from river beds. At several places, the soil is loamy and makes cultivation unprofitable. Khadar soils are present in relatively low-lying areas, which are subject to occasional flooding, and, therefore, get freshly deposited silt, which enhances their fertility and permits growing of excellent Rabi crops.

(vi) Saline and Alkali Soil

Soils which have excessive proportions of soluble salts and/or exchangeable sodium, due to which crop production is seriously hampered, are locally known as "Reh/Usar". They have a high soil pH value. There is a deficiency of calcium, nitrogen and micro-nutrients like zinc, extremely low water intake rate and hydraulic conductivity, resulting in poor moisture transmission characteristics. The presence of calcium carbonate nodules, called Kankar, often occurring at almost 1 metre depth, and poor physical condition, lead to hindrance in root penetration. Soils of this type are observed in almost all villages of the block.

1.10.7 Natural Vegetation

Amethi Block has an almost inhabited human occupance for over three millenia, and centuries of plough and pastoral culture has reduced the natural vegetation, except in pockets of the Tarai and some river banks. With a moderate and healthy climate and fertile soil, the district flora presents no peculiarities. Patches of Dhak (*Butea frondosa*) are found here and there. The district, in general, is well wooded and contains magnificent groves of mango, Jamun (*Eugenia jambolana*) and Mahua (*Bassia latifolia*).

References

1. Gedroiz KK, Saline soils and their improvement, *J exp Agron*, **18** (1977) (In Russian; translated by Waksman SA).
2. Sharma HS, *Ravine erosion in India* (Concept Publishing Co., New Delhi) 1980.
3. Singh Abha Lakshmi, *Economics and geography of agricultural land reclamation* (BR Publishing Corp, Vivekanand Nagar, New Delhi) 1978.
4. Yadav HR, *Genesis and utilization of wastelands* (Concept Publishing Co., New Delhi) 1986.
5. Dhir RP, Concept and definition of wastelands, *Proc ICAR Sponsored Summer Institute* (Central Arid Zone Research Institute, Jodhpur) 1986.
6. Sarkar Vinod, Vegetation of semi-arid wastelands and indicators of degradation, *Proc ICAR Sponsored Summer Institute* (Central Arid Zone Research Institute, Jodhpur) 1986.
7. Sen AK, Typology of wastelands and mapping procedure in Rajasthan, *Proc ICAR Sponsored Summer Institute* (Central Arid Zone Research Institute, Jodhpur) 1986.

8. Saxena SK, Economic attributes of some multipurpose plants needed for wasteland development, *Proc ICAR Sponsored Summer Institute* (Central Arid Zone Research Institute, Jodhpur) 1986.
9. Chopra DP, Promising horticultural plants of economic importance for wastelands, *Proc ICAR Sponsored Summer Institute* (Central Arid Zone Research Institute, Jodhpur) 1986.
10. Shankarnarayan KA, Agroforestry, the key to rehabilitation of wasteland, *Proc ICAR Sponsored Summer Institute* (Central Arid Zone Research Institute, Jodhpur), 1986.
11. Mittal JP, Role of livestock farming in wasteland development, *Proc ICAR Sponsored Summer Institute* (Central Arid Zone Research Institute, Jodhpur) 1986.
12. Dhir RP, Organisations involved or concerned in development of wasteland, *Proc ICAR Sponsored Summer Institute* (Central Arid Zone Research Institute, Jodhpur) 1986.
13. Verma Balvir, Principles and practices in gully reclamation, *Proc ICAR Sponsored Summer Institute* (Central Arid Zone Research Institute, Jodhpur) 1986.
14. Chinnamani S, Forestry, social forestry and agroforestry in ravine reclamation, *Proc ICAR Sponsored Summer Institute* (Central Arid Zone Research Institute, Jodhpur) 1986.
15. Singh RP, Dryland agriculture and wasteland development, *Proc ICAR Sponsored Summer Institute* (Central Arid Zone Research Institute, Jodhpur) 1986.
16. Bhumbla DR, Note on reclamation of alkali soils in Uttar Pradesh, *Proc Seminar-cum-Workshop on Afforestation of Usar Wastelands* (Society for Promotion of Wasteland Development, New Delhi) 1985.
17. Pant SC, Rols of NABARD in reclamation of usar wasteland, *Proc Seminar-cum-Workshop on Afforestation of Usar Wastelands* (Society for Promotion of Wasteland Development, New Delhi) 1985.
18. Aggarwal VP, Background note on reclamation of alkali area usar lands of Uttar Pradesh, *Proc Seminar-cum-*

Workshop on Afforestation of Usar Wastelands (Society for Promotion of Wasteland Development) New Delhi) 1985.

19. Khanduri HC, Reclamation of usar land for agriculture by afforestation, *Proc Seminar-cum-Workshop on Afforestation of Usar Wastelands* (Society for Promotion of Wasteland Development, New Delhi) 1985.
20. Shrivastava KB, Role of prosopis in wastelands development, *Proc Seminar-cum-Workshop on Afforestation of Usar Wastelands* (Society for Promotion of Wasteland Development, New Delhi) 1985.
21. Hegde NG, Wasteland development: Alternatives to *Prospois juliflora*, *Proc Seminar-cum-Workshop on Afforestation of Usar Wastelands* (Society for Promotion of Wasteland Development, New Delhi) 1985.
22. Sharma K, Prospects of integrating agroforestry with goat husbandry for economic upliftment of rural poor in wastelands of India, *Proc Seminar-cum-Workshop on Afforestation of Usar Wastelands* (Society for Promotion of Wasteland Development, New Delhi) 1985.
23. Mastafa K Tolba, *Rolling back the wasteland*, Lecture delivered at a meet organized by the Society for Promotion of Wasteland Development, India International Centre, New Delhi, 27 December 1982.
24. Bhumbla DR & Khare Arvind, Estimate of Wastelands in India, in *Wastelands diagnosis and treatment*, edited by HR Yadav (Concept Publishing Co, New Delhi), 1986.
25. Sen AK, Land utilization mapping to estimate the wastelands of arid zone by photo-interpretation technique, in *Wasteland diagnosis and treatment*, edited by HR Yadav (Concept Publishing Co, New Delhi) 1986.
26. Shankarnarayan KA, Sen AK & Balakram, Analysis of wastelands in arid zone by remote sensing techniques, in *Wasteland diagnosis and treatment*, edited by HR Yadav (Concept Publishing Co, New Delhi) 1980.
27. Banerjee AK, Reclamation of wastelands in laterite tracts of Eastern India, in *Wasteland diagnosis and treatment*, edited by HR Yadav (Concept Publishing Co, New Delhi), 1986, 113-22.

28. Abrol IP & Joshi PK, Economic viability of reclamation of alkali lands with special reference to agriculture and forestry, in *Wasteland diagnosis and treatment*, edited by HR Yadav (Concept Publishing Co., New Delhi), 1986, 149-68.
29. Mathur RK, Economics of agroforestry for wasteland reclamation, in *Wasteland diagnosis and treatment*, edited by HR Yadav (Concept Publishing Co., New Delhi), 1986, 175-87.
30. Shah Parmesh, Economics of wasteland development projects undertaken by Gujarat State Rural Development Corporation, in *Wasteland diagnosis and treatment*, edited by HR Yadav (Concept Publishing Co., 1986, New Delhi), 189-213.
31. Venkataraman KG, Designing, planning and financing of tree plantation projects over state lands, in *Wasteland diagnosis and treatment*, edited by HR Yadav (Concept Publishing Co., New Delhi), 1986, 221-25.
32. Chowdhary Kamala, Forestry development: Strategy & structure, in *Wasteland diagnosis and treatment*, edited by HR Yadav (Concept Publishing Co., New Delhi) 1986, 227-41.
33. *The Imperial Gazette of India*, **33**(1974) 130-37.
34. Singh M, *Land utilisation in Eastern Uttar Pradesh*, PhD thesis, AMU, Aligarh.
35. Wadia DN, *Geology of India* (London), 1953, 385.
36. Krishnan MS, *Geology of India and Burma* (Madras) 1960.
37. Glennie EA, Gravity anomalies in the structure of earth's crust, *Mem geol Soc India, Prof. Pap. No. 29*, 1932, 22.
38. Blandfor HF, Rainfall of India, *Mem Indian met Dep*, **33** (1985–86) 130.
39. Clark KGT, The vicissitudes of the summer rainfall of the Indo-Gangetic Plain and the valley, *Geography*, **17**(1932) 288.
40. Shafi M, *Land utilisation in Eastern Uttar Pradesh*, PhD thesis, Aligarh Muslim University, Aligarh, 1960, 40-41.

2

Distribution of Wastelands

2.1 Introduction

Wastelands are not a new phenomenon. The term was used for common lands usually with less fertile soil, which failed to give any return to the medieval cultivators. A layman may define wasteland as land lying uninhabited and uncultivated and which is no longer serving any purpose. The adjective waste has now disappeared, because in many cases these common lands are much valued as open spaces. Stamp[1] appropriately defined wasteland as "Land which has been previously used but which has been abandoned and no further use has been found for it". A broad definition for wasteland would be "Land which is uncultivable or is presently lying unutilized due to different constraints but had been used previously, which is giving very low actual return, i.e., has low economic potential, is ecologically unstable, or whose top soil has completely lost its fertility status, which has developed toxicity and is, therefore, unfit for the growth of crops and trees due to environmental or anthropogenic problems, has been abandoned and no further use has been found for it".

2.2 Types of Wastelands

In the present study, the classification of wastelands was done on the basis of the land use classification proposed by the Directorate of Economics and Statistics, Ministry of Agriculture. The cultivable wastelands of Amethi were thus classified into the following broad categories: Waterlogged, usar, banjar and other types. Fallows other than current fallow were further sub-divided into old fallow (2-5 years) and fallow (1-2 years) lands. Thus, in Amethi Block, six types of wastelands have been derived from two important categories of land use, viz., culturable waste and fallows other than current fallow. Wastelands of all above types exist in Amethi and are discussed below.

(i) Waterlogged Land

Waterlogged land is that where the water table is at or near the earth's surface and water stands for most of the year and soil pores in the root zones of the crop get saturated with water which inhibits the growth and activity of plants. As a result such lands are left uncultivated.

(ii) Usar Land

Those fluffy soils which have a whitish or greyish appearance deposited on the surface and are not easily cultivable. They are commonly known as reh, rehar or usar.

Lands which have excessive proportions of soluble salts due to which crop production is seriously hampered are known as salt-affected soils; locally they are known as usar lands.

(iii) Banjar Land

These are lands which were taken up for cultivation but are presently out of cultivation for a period of not less than five years. These lands are left uncultivated for long periods.

(iv) Old Fallow Land

These are lands which were under cultivation, but presently are out of cultivation for a period of not less than two years and not more than five years.

(v) Fallow Lands

These are lands which can be taken up for cultivation but are temporarily out of cultivation for not less than one year and not more than two years.

(vi) Other Types of Wastelands

Other types of wastelands include lands which cannot as per definition be put under any of the above heads. They are mentioned in the village handbook. The other types of wastelands are those which were under cultivation but are presently left out of cultivation for one reason or the other.

2.3 Distribution of Wastelands

In Sultanpur District, wastelands constituted as much as 12.85% of its total area in 1977-78. By 1981-82, their area had increased by 10.93% in comparison to that in 1977-78, coming to 13.72% of the total area of the district. By 1986-87, their area had further increased by 3.35% to reach a level of 14.18% of the total area. Data showing the proportional distribution of different categories of wastelands are given in Table 2.1. It is seen that the increase during the period 1981-82 to 1986-87 has not been as pronounced as during 1977-78 to 1981-82.

Study of the distribution of wastelands of Sultanpur District indicated that banjar land forms the largest component—3.93% of the total area of the district in 1977-78, 4.18% in 1981-82 and 4.32% in 1986-87. The proportions of the other categories are in the following descending order: Fallow land, usar land, ravine land, waterlogged land and kankrili land. Kankrili land forms less than 0.1% of the total area. The growth in the area from 1981-82 to 1986-87 has been maximum in the case of ravine land (15.09%) followed by kankrili land, waterlogged and old fallow land. There has been negligible growth in the area of fallow land. There has been a significant change in area of all wasteland types at district level, but this change had become marginal by 1986-87,

Table 2.1 — Data on Wastelands in Sultanpur District

Sl No.	Wasteland type	% of total area of the district			% growth from 1977-78 to 1981–82	% growth from 1981-82 to 1986-87
		1977-78	1981-82	1986-87		
1	Waterlogged land	0.43	0.58	0.65	29.96	12.06
2	Usar land	0.46	0.54	0.59	15.79	9.25
3	Banjar land	3.93	4.18	4.32	19.48	3.35
4	Old fallow land	1.35	1.51	1.67	11.68	10.60
5	Fallow land	2.73	2.94	2.99	7.92	1.70
6	Kankrili land	0.06	0.07	0.08	15.50	14.28
7	Ravine land	0.43	0.53	0.61	16.47	15.09
8	Other types of wasteland	3.14	3.43	3.73	9.03	8.74
	Total wasteland	12.85	13.72	14.18	10.93	3.35

Table 2.2—Data on Wastelands in Amethi Block

Sl No.	Wasteland type	% of total area of block in			% growth from 1977-78 to 1981-82	% growth from 1981-82 to 1986-87
		1977-78	1981-82	1986-87		
1	Waterlogged land	0.17	0.22	0.27	33.82	22.72
2	Usar land	0.34	0.35	0.28	2.17	—20.00
3	Banjar land	2.50	2.57	2.78	2.96	8.17
4	Old fallow land	0.62	0.71	0.83	13.43	16.90
5	Fallow land	3.00	3.25	3.41	8.13	4.92
6	Other types of wastelands	2.05	2.29	2.36	11.67	3.06
	Total wastelands	8.64	9.32	9.71	9.92	4.18

because most of the wastelands are now being afforested or being put to industrial uses. In most of the cases, the farmers have become conscious of the benefits of reclaiming wastelands and have started putting them to diverse uses.

In Amethi Block, wastelands constituted 8.64% of the total area in 1977-78, which increased to 9.32% in 1981-82 and to 9.71% in 1986-87 (Table 2.2). There has been 9 92% increase in the area of wasteland from 1977-78 to 1981-82. The growth from 1981-82 to 1986-87 is 4.18%, which shows that there is a positive change. This shows that some of the wastelands are now being utilized for different purposes as a result of which their further growth has been checked.

It is seen from the data on distribution of wastelands in Amethi Block over different categories that in 1977-78, fallow land had the highest proportion (3.00%), followed by banjar land (2.50%), other types of wastelands (2.05%), old fallow land (0.62%), usar land (0.34%) and waterlogged land (0.17%). There was an increase in the area of wastelands in Amethi during 1977-78 to 1981-82; in 1981-82, the area of fallow land in the Block was higher (3.25%) in comparison to areas of other categories of wastelands. By 1881-82, the area of banjar land had increased to 2.59% followed by other types of wasteland (2.29%), old fallow land (0.71%), usar land (0.35%) and waterlogged land (0.22%). In 1986–87, the proportion of fallow land was highest (3.41%) followed by banjar land (2.78%), other types of wastelands (2.36%), old fallow land (0.83%), usar land (0.28%) and waterlogged land (0.27%). It is evident that the areas of all wasteland types have increased in both half decadal years, i.e. 1977-78 to 1981-82 and 1981-82 to 1986-87. The percentage of wastelands is lower for the period 1981-82 to 1986-17 in comparison to that for 1977–78 to 1981-82, because in most of the areas such wastelands are now utilized for various purposes and their further growth is being checked.

The overall increase in the area of wastelands in Amethi Block during 1977-78 to 1981-82 has taken place for waterlogged land (33.82%) because of over-irrigation with canal water, mismanagement of water and accumulation of rainy water in low-lying areas in the absence of outlets. Next to waterlogged land, old fallow land has shown the highest percentage increase (13.43%) followed by other types of wastelands (11.67%), fallow land (8.13%), banjar land (2.96%) and usar land (2.17%). During 1981-82 to 1986-87, the overall increase in the area of wastelands was 4.18%, which is much lower than that for the period 1977-78 to 1981–82. The highest growth during this period has been in respect of waterlogged land (22.72%) followed by old fallow land (16.90%), banjar land (8.17%), fallow land (4.92%) and other types of wastelands (3.06%); all these increases are comparatively lower than those for the period 1977-78 to 1981-82. For usar land, there has been a negative change (—20.00%) due to the fact that most of the usar land has been planted under the various afforestation schemes; in addition, it is being utilized for industrial and other purposes.

2.4 Village Level Distribution of Wastelands

Distribution of various wasteland types in Amethi Block at village level for 1986-87 was studied on the basis of maps and digital information collected during the field work, personal interaction with the village accountants, village development officers and villagers, and by examining the Milan Khasara available in the revenue office at Tehsil Headquarters.

(i) Waterlogged Land

Data on distribution of waterlogged land at village level are given in Table 2.3 and Map 3. A very high proportion of waterlogged land as percentage of the total area (1.61-2.00%) is seen in the villages Naraini and Katra Hulasi, Bandupur and Jairampur due to surface accumulation of both rain water and canal irrigation water. The affected land is low-lying. There is no outlet due to which water accumulates; continuous accumulation of water has also affected the surrounding areas. The proportion of waterlogged lands is at intermediate level (0.81-1.20%) in Kohara, Maharajpur, Ramgarh, Katara Himmat Singh, Brahimpur and Jangal Ramnagar and at low level (0.41-0.80%) in Kakwa, Sultanpur,

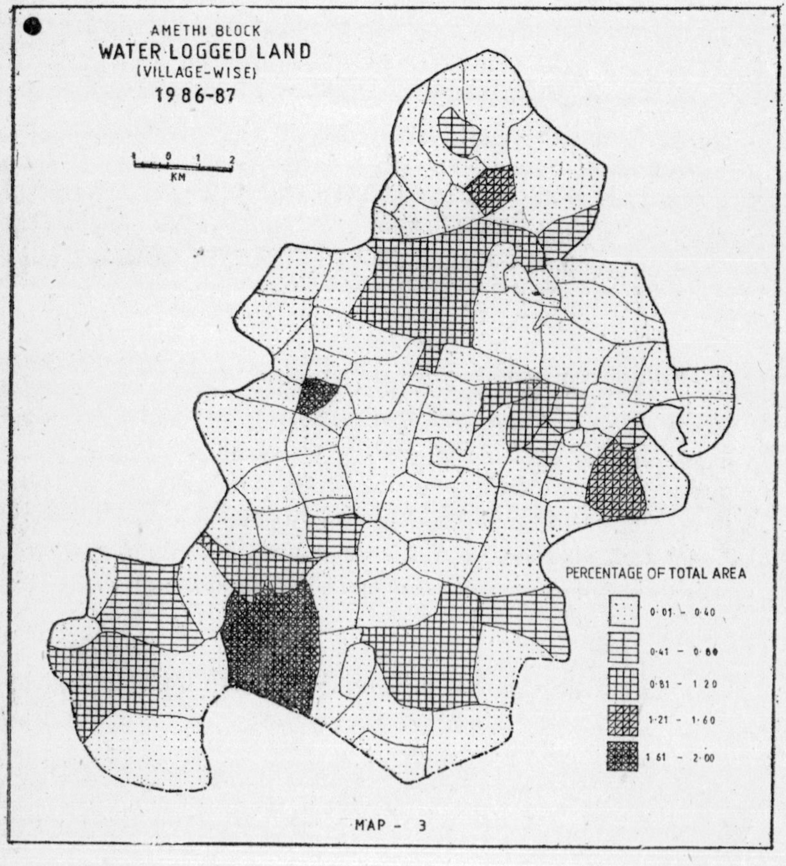
AMETHI BLOCK
WATER LOGGED LAND
(VILLAGE-WISE)
1986-87
1 0 1 2
KM
PERCENTAGE OF TOTAL AREA
0·01 - 0·40
0·41 - 0·80
0·81 - 1·20
1·21 - 1·60
1·61 - 2·00

MAP - 3

Table 2.3—Distribution of Wastelands in Amethi over Different Categories for 1986-87

(Values represent area in %)

Sl No.	Name of village	Water-logged	Usar land	Banjar land	Old fallow land	Fallow land	Other types of wasteland	Total waste-land
(1)	(2)	(3)	(4)	(5)	(6)	(7)	(8)	(9)
1	Trilokpur	0.02	6.47	3.36	0.05	0.96	0.72	11.51
2	Teri	0.01	0.04	0.50	0.03	0.25	0.50	1.25
3	Laukipur	0.50	3.01	0.75	0.25	0.76	0.26	7.52
4	Katara Maharani	0.01	0.21	1.18	2.95	4.13	2.36	10.62
5	Sarai Khema	0.01	2.29	0.86	1.72	10.05	0.61	14.92
6	Dandupur	1.30	0.29	0.29	0.33	8.07	1.06	11.41
7	Bhupatpur	0.01	0.31	1.80	0.06	3.00	1.20	6.01
8	Ramdaipur	0.31	0.61	1.36	0.46	0.31	0.46	3.20
9	Naugwana	0.01	0.02	2.23	0.01	2.97	2.23	7.43
10	Wahapur	0.30	0.01	2.01	0.08	0.47	2.32	4.63

(Contd.)

Table 2.3—*Contd.*

1	2	3	4	5	6	7	8	9
11	Jangal Tikari	0.01	0.07	1.50	0.09	0.61	8.38	9.38
12	Bhaganpur	0.18	0.38	1.21	1.28	0.73	4.26	7.24
13	Tala	0.01	0.08	1.19	0.03	0.96	0.92	3.06
14	Kushi Thali	0.01	0.18	2.16	0.10	1.25	2.86	6.55
15	Jangal Ram Nagar	0.85	0.85	1.02	2.83	1.92	3.43	10.90
16	Mahmudpur	0.01	0.10	3.84	1.80	0.38	4.16	10.18
17	Ramnagar Mati	0.02	1.09	0.52	0.06	11.43	0.52	13.56
18	Marafapur	0.03	3.19	3.09	0.08	5.15	2.06	23.50
19	Walipur	0.03	0.21	1.14	1.10	2.01	3.41	7.66
20	Basuwapur	0.51	0.38	1.21	1.80	0.32	6.04	9.56
21	Benipur	0.31	1.30	2.56	0.37	1.12	4.86	10.52
22	Pursawna	0.02	0.05	3.12	1.14	0.83	5.71	10.80
23	Ramnathpur	0.04	0.03	2.96	0.59	1.18	4.79	9.47
24	Sarai Rajshah	0.14	2.81	1.35	2.70	0.81	4.01	11.82
25	Parsauli	0.03	0.53	2.86	3.81	1.33	3.72	12.25

26	Katrafulkunwar	0.20	0.87	1.17	0.18	3.50	3.18	9.33
27	Jagi Patti	0.02	0.09	2.32	0.23	2.06	6.19	10.57
28	Hathkila	0.01	0.19	2.05	4.12	5.14	1.93	13.43
29	Jamalpatti	0.71	2.17	3.26	2.07	1.22	2.38	12.71
30	Kherauna	0.03	0.89	1.08	0.17	1.43	4.12	7.52
31	Manipur Radho	0.04	3.12	2.85	0.93	2.45	3.78	13.13
32	Mandharpatti	0.15	1.62	3.28	1.21	3.72	1.07	11.05
33	Chachakapur	0.74	2.21	3.01	2.02	1.35	6.19	8.99
34	Brahimpur	1.12	0.39	2.14	0.56	2.79	2.23	9.23
35	Sarwanpur	0.01	2.13	1.82	0.81	3.16	5.48	12.59
36	Katara Raja	1.18	0.78	2.15	3.12	2.73	3.19	13.15
37	Waria Rampur	0.12	1.20	1.83	0.33	2.38	1.67	7.20
38	Bharathipur	0.02	2.86	2.03	2.59	2.88	3.93	12.29
39	Lonipur	0.82	0.18	3.94	2.09	2.86	3.73	13.44
40	Raipurfulwari	0.18	1.25	3.27	1.78	2.16	2.03	10.67
41	Nuwanawa	0.01	0.44	1.06	3.18	1.15	0.27	6.10

(Contd.)

Table 2.3—*(Contd.)*

1	2	3	4	5	6	7	8	9
42	Umappurganpatti	0.01	2.85	1.71	0.34	3.58	4.25	12.39
43	Katara Hulasi	0.02	1.12	2.38	1.19	0.68	3.15	8.42
44	Sundarpur	0.03	1.08	3.84	0.89	1.74	2.86	10.41
45	Ahiraval	1.80	0.08	2.86	1.83	0.81	3.74	11.04
46	Haripur	0.16	1.72	0.85	1.23	0.81	2.34	7.11
47	Loharata	0.01	2.34	1.18	2.27	0.16	3.28	11.75
48	Sonpur Mankanth	0.02	0.37	3.14	3.81	1.82	2.97	12.11
49	Darakha	0.38	1.26	2.18	1.67	3.76	1.32	10.57
50	Sarai Hirmati	0.03	0.16	0.83	1.24	3.78	2.85	8.70
51	Agahar	0.01	0.39	1.31	0.17	2.45	6.23	10.38
52	Biyasiya	0.02	0.93	2.87	1.25	3.86	4.35	13.26
53	Maharajpur	0.86	3.81	1.09	2.83	2.12	2.31	13.02
54	Chaturbhujapur	0.28	1.39	2.59	1.18	3.11	2.58	11.13
55	Mohwa	0.03	1.82	2.79	1.34	0.13	3.80	9.75
56	Jhauneo	0.02	0.67	1.82	2.37	1.45	2.76	9.67

57	Sultanpur	0.02	1.08	1.98	2.87	0.73	3.42	10.08
58	Purabgaon	0.12	1.51	3.09	0.19	1.81	1.63	8.17
59	Pirthipur	0.02	1.02	1.22	0.84	2.16	3.36	8.60
60	Gaderi	0.74	2.18	1.04	1.63	0.16	1.48	7.06
61	Dhandhudhar	0.01	0.05	3.23	2.79	3.78	2.61	12.41
62	Korari Girdhar Shah	0.01	0.88	1.25	0.93	2.13	3.18	8.37
63	Mangalpur	0.01	0.36	2.80	0.09	1.37	5.09	9.62
64	Gangauli	0.01	1.24	2.61	0.12	2.84	3.79	10.48
65	Ramdevpur	0.67	2.13	1.07	3.67	0.17	2.48	10.02
66	Rebha	0.01	1.92	2.16	2.73	1.10	2.64	11.55
67	Gyanchandpur	0.02	1.62	3.28	1.21	3.72	1.07	10.90
68	Mahaso	0.03	0.48	1.86	0.16	2.51	3.86	8.74
69	Jairampur	1.22	0.91	1.36	1.96	1.38	2.67	9.50
70	Dedhpasar	0.16	1.32	2.84	1.82	2.68	4.81	13.63
71	Bhusahari	0.68	2.81	1.52	0.86	2.13	1.32	9.38
72	Himmatgarh	0.03	1.02	1.13	3.18	1.21	1.02	7.56

(Contd.)

Table 2.3—*Contd.*

1	2	3	4	5	6	7	8	9
73	Dehara	0.23	0.14	3.66	1.81	1.57	2.70	9.97
74	Rajapurkohara	0.01	1.62	3.12	0.19	1.05	0.53	6.32
75	Kudwa Mahmudpur	0.01	0.31	3.64	1.87	2.73	1.36	9.66
76	Ramgarh	1.12	2.01	1.02	0.29	4.02	1.66	10.42
77	Baratali	0.03	2.86	2.03	0.59	2.88	3.93	12.29
78	Nainaha	0.04	1.02	2.03	0.32	0.87	1.74	0.65
79	Naraini	1.59	1.28	3.74	0.76	0.21	3.12	10.10
80	Saraiya Duban	0.13	3.72	2.09	2.29	2.01	1.02	13.04
81	Muhammadpur	0.05	1.20	2.18	1.70	0.18	2.45	7.52
82	Kohara	1.06	0.17	0.92	2.12	3.06	2.16	9.32
83	Kakwa	0.76	1.85	1.38	0.37	4.23	2.86	11.45
84	Saidpur	0.06	3.81	1.01	0.98	1.72	3.45	10.89
85	Dalshahpur	0.10	1.31	2.58	1.34	2.68	3.62	12.03

Bhasahari, Sarwanpur, Chachakpur, Jamalpatti, Basuwapur and Laukipur. It is very low(<0.40%) in the rest of the villages. Very low percentage of waterlogged land is found more in the central, northern and eastern parts of the block. because these villages are less affected by the excessive accumulation of surface water and most of the villages are having outlets for the accumulated water. The overall proportion of waterlogged lands at village level in Amethi Block is low. Even this can be checked and the lands reclaimed by constructing drains as outlets for the accumulated surface rain/irrigation water and through proper management of irrigation water.

(ii) Usar Land

The proportion of usar land in Amethi Block villages varies from 0.07% to 6.47%. Very high percentage of usar land is seen in village Trilokpur (6.47%) located in the northern part of the block (Map 4). It is at intermediate level (2.81–4.20%) in Marafanagar, Sarai Rajshah, Bharathipur, Umapur-ganapatti, Saidpur, Saraiyaduban, Baratali and Bhusahari. Because of high pH value of the soil, this land is left uncultivated. High salinity of the soil prevents survival of plants. There is relatively low distribution of usar land (2.81-4.20%) in Rajpurkohara, Ramgarh, Gaderi, Purabgaon, Mochwa, Gyanchandpur, Rebha, Chachakapur, Sarwanpur, Loharata, Haripur and Saraikhema. Very low percentage of usar land (<1.40%) is seen in most other villages which fall in the central and northern parts of the block. Of course, all the villages of the block are affected by the usarization problem to varying extents.

(iii) Banjar Land

The proportion of banjar land in the villages of Amethi Block varies from 0.29 to 3.94%. Very high proportion of banjar land (3.21-4.00%) is seen in Dehra, Kudwa Mahmudpur, Naraini, Dhandhudhar, Sunderpur, Lonipur, Raipur Fulwari, Mahmudpur and Trilokpur and very high (2.91-

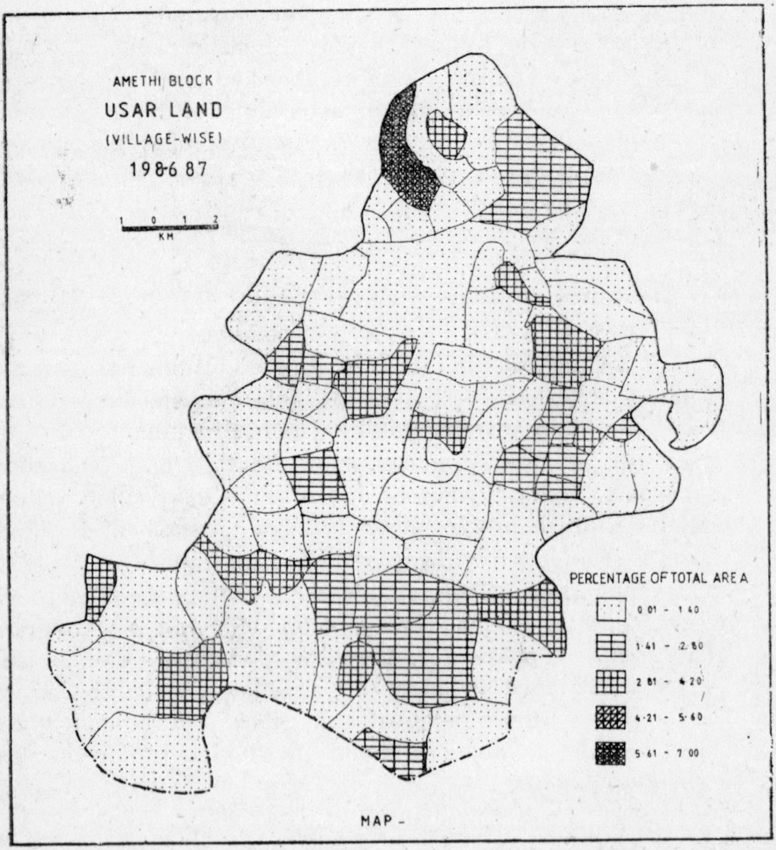

AMETHI BLOCK
USAR LAND
(VILLAGE-WISE)
1986 87
1 0 1 2
KM
PERCENTAGE OF TOTAL AREA
0.01 - 1.40
1.41 - 2.80
2.81 - 4.20
4.21 - 5.60
5.61 - 7.00
MAP -

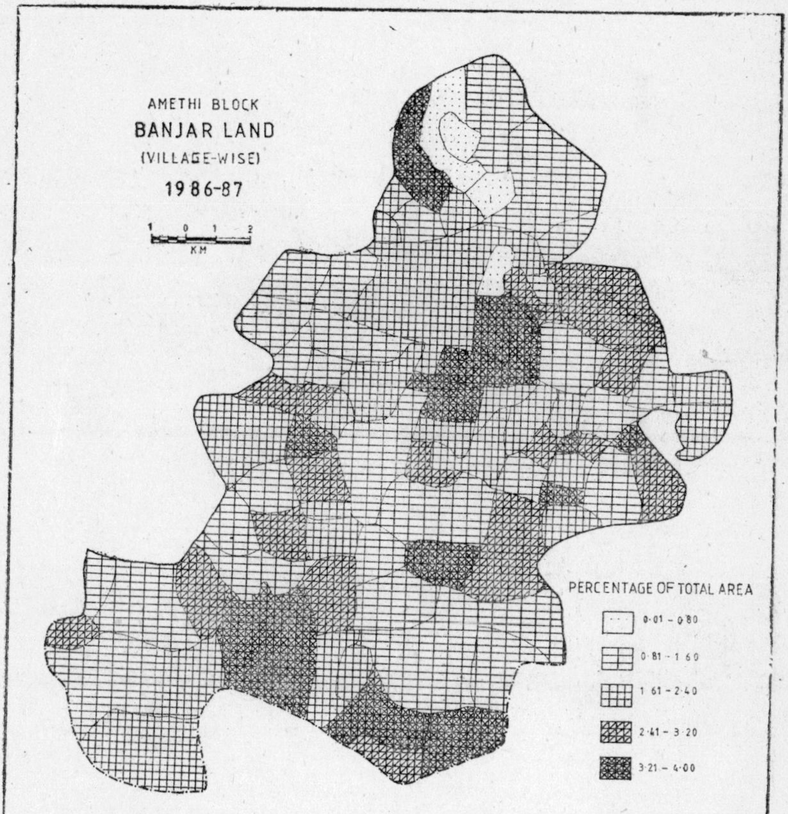
AMETHI BLOCK
BANJAR LAND
(VILLAGE-WISE)
1986-87
1 0 1 2
KM
PERCENTAGE OF TOTAL AREA
0·01 – 0·80
0·81 – 1·60
1·61 – 2·40
2·41 – 3·20
3·21 – 4·00

MAP - 5

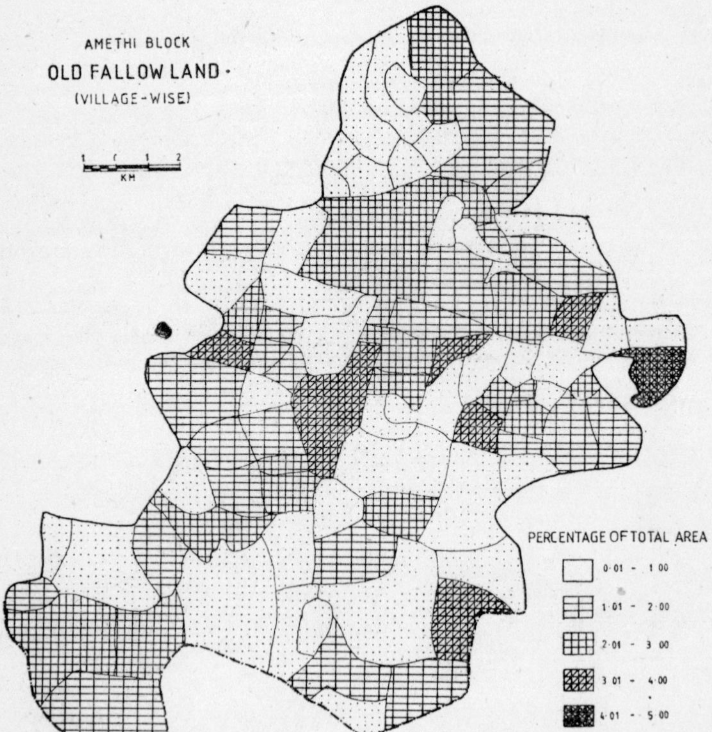
AMETHI BLOCK
OLD FALLOW LAND
(VILLAGE-WISE)
KM
PERCENTAGE OF TOTAL AREA
0·01 - 1·00
1·01 - 2·00
2·01 - 3·00
3·01 - 4·00
4·01 - 5·00

MAP - 6

3.20%) in Rajpurkohra, Dalshahpur, Biyasiya, Maharajpur, Mochwa, Sonpur Mankanth, Katara Hulasi, Gangauli, Mangalpur, Dedhpusar Chachakapur, Parsauli, Pursawna, Benipur and Marafanagar. The banjar lands of these villages are not utilized for any purpose and are left uncultivated for more than 5 years due to their low fertility status. Banjar lands occur at intermediate level (1.61-2.40%) in Muhammadpur, Saraiyaduban, Darakha, Variarampur, Bharathipur, Katara Himmatsingh, Brahimpur, Mahaso, Hathkila, Jagipatti and Jangalramnagar. Their proportion is low (0.81-1.60%) in Kohra, Kakwa, Saidpur, Maharajpur Agahar, Saraihirmati, Nuwanwa, Korarigirdharshah, Pirthipur, Ramgarh, Himmatgarh, Gaderi, Ramdevpur. Sairampur, Kherauna, Persauli, Sarairajshah, Tola, Bhaganpur, Kushithali, Loharate, Haripur, Tala, Bhaganpur, Jangaltikari, Katara Mehrani, Saraikhema, Basuwapur and Katarafulkunwar. Very low percentage (<0.80%) of banjar land is seen in Laukipur, Teri Dandupur and Ramnagar Mafi.

(iv) Old Fallow Land

Very high percentage (4.01-5.00%) of old fallow land is seen in village Hathkila, while it is fairly high (3.01-4.00%) in Himmatgarh, Ramdevpur, Nauwanwa, Sonpur Mankanth, Katara Himmat Singh and Parsauli (Map 6). The proportion is at intermediate level (2.01-3.00%) in Kohra, Saraiy Duban, Maharajpur, Sultanpur, Jhaunei, Dhandhudhar, Sarwanpur, Jamalpatti, Bharathipur, Loniapur, Loharata, Jangalramnagar, Sarairaj Shah and Katara Mahrani, and at low level (1.01-2.00%) in Muhammadpur, Dalshahpur, Kudwamahmudpur. Dehra, Gaderi, Darkha, Sarai Hiramati, Maharajpur, Mochwa, Haripur, Katara Hulsi, Bhaganpur, Raipur Fulwari, Mahmudpur, Dehhpasar, Jairampur, Pursawna, Basuwapur and Sarai Khema. In villages in the south eastern and north western parts of the block, the proportion of old fallow lands is very low (<1%). The old fallow lands of these villages were left out of cultivation for more than 2 years but less than 5 years due to the low fertility status of the soil. The idea behind this is to allow these lands to regenerate.

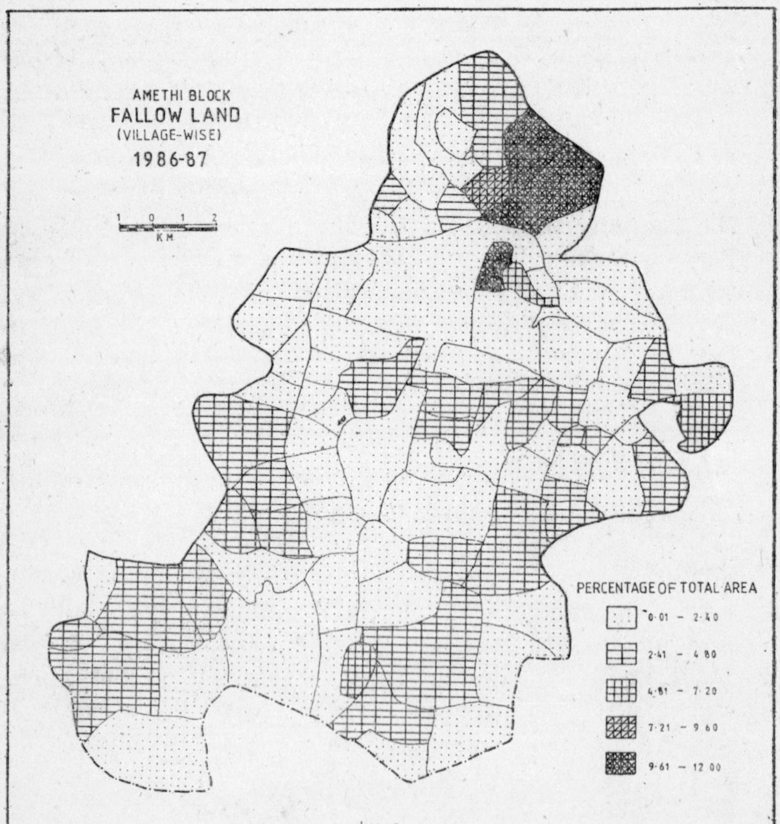
AMETHI BLOCK
FALLOW LAND
(VILLAGE-WISE)
1986-87
1 0 1 2
KM
PERCENTAGE OF TOTAL AREA
0·01 – 2·40
2·41 – 4·80
4·81 – 7·20
7·21 – 9·60
9·61 – 12·00

MAP

(v) Fallow Land

Very high percentage (9.61-12.00%) of fallow land is found in the villages Saraikhema and Ramnagar Mafi, and fairly high percentage (7.21-9.60%) in village Dandupur (Map 7). It is at intermediate level (4.81-7.20%) in Baratali, Marafanagar and Hathkila and at low level (2 41-4.80%) in Kohra, Dalshahpur, Kakwa, Agahar, Mahrajpur, Sarai Hirmati, Darakha, Unapurganpeth, Raipurfulwari, Katara Himmat Singh Brahimpur, Sarwanpur, Dendupur, Ramgarh, Kudwamahmud-pur, Gangauli, Mahaso Gyanchandpur, Rebha, Dedhasar, Katara Fulkunwar, Wahapur, Bhupatpur, Katara Maharani and Marafanagar. The rest of the villages have very little (<2.40%) of fallow land. These fallow lands are left uncultivated for more than a year but less than two years for some reason or the other.

(vi) Other Types of Wastelands

Very high percentage (7.21-9.00%) of other types of wastelands is observed in village Jangal Tikari, and fairly high percentage (5.41-7.20%) in Agahar, Chachakapur, Sarwanpur, Jagipatti, Pursawna and Basuwapur (Map 8). It is at inter-mediate level (3 61-5.40%) in Dalshahpur, Biyasiya, Mochwa, Baratali Gangauli, Mahso, Dedhpasar, Rebha Kherauna, Katara-ful Kunwar, Sarairajshah, Mangolpur, Bharathipur, Lonipur, Umapur Ganapatti, Tala and Benipur, and at low level (1.81-3.60%) in Muhammadpur, Kohra, Kokwa, Saidpur, Naraini, Maharajpur, Saraihimmati, Sultanpur, Jhaunei, Dehra, Ramgarh, Pisthipur, Dhandhudhur, Korarigirdharshah, Sunderpur, Sonpur Mankenth, Loharat, Nauganwa, Loharata, Kushithali, Jangal-ramnagar, Raipurfulwari, Katarhimmatsingh, Jairampur, Hathkila, Laukipur and Kataramaharani. The proportion of other types of wastelands is very low (<1.80%) in Saraiya Duban, Rajpur Kohra, Kudwamahmuddpur, Nainaha, Purab-gaon, Gaderi, Himmatgarh, Bhushaputi, Gyanchandpur, Waria-rampur, Newanwa, Darakha, Ramnagar Mafi, Ramdaipur, Bhapatpur, Dandupur, Saraikhema, Teri and Trilokpur.

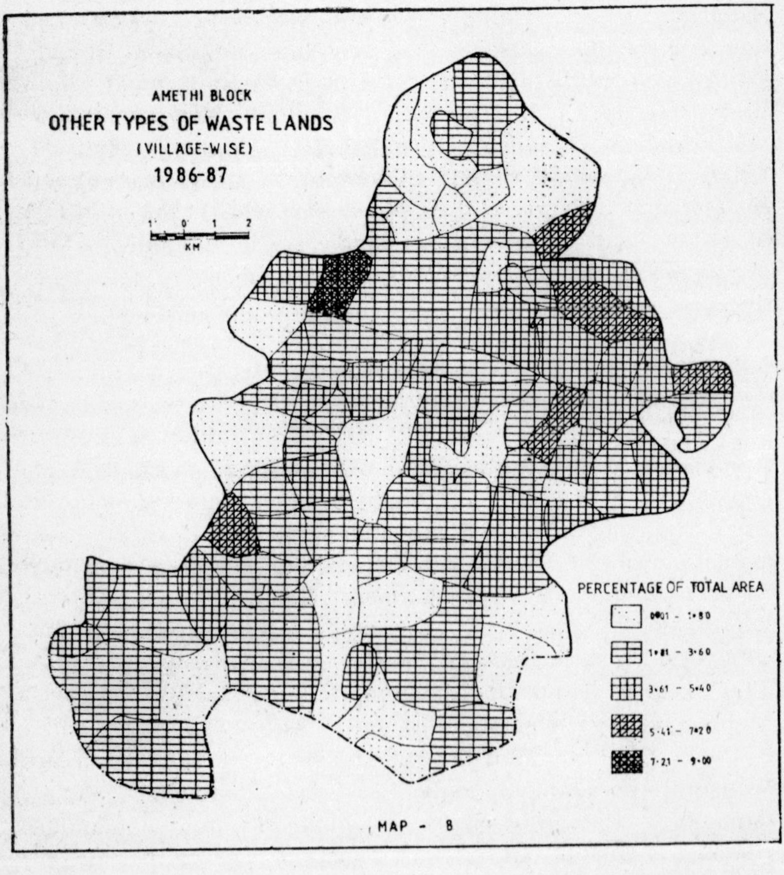
AMETHI BLOCK
OTHER TYPES OF WASTE LANDS
(VILLAGE-WISE)
1986-87
1 0 1 2
KM
PERCENTAGE OF TOTAL AREA
0·01 - 1·80
1·81 - 3·60
3·61 - 5·40
5·41 - 7·20
7·21 - 9·00

MAP - 8

(vii) Total Wastelands

The proportion of wastelands in the block at village level goes up to 15% of total area (Map 9). Very high percentage (12.01-15.00%) of total wastelands is seen in Saraiyaduban, Dalshahpur, Biyasiya, Maharajpur, Baratali, Dhandhudhar, Dedhpasar, Hathkila, Bharathipur, Loniapur, Katarhimmatsingh, Unapurganapatti Rersauli, Ramnagar Mafi, Marafanagar and Saraikhema. It is fairly high (9.01-12.00%) in Kohra, Kakwa, Saidpur, Naraini, Agahar, Maharajpur, Sultanpur, Dehra, Kudwamahmudpur, Ramgarh, Bhusahari, Gangauli, Ramdevpur Chachakapur, Rebha, Sairampur, Katarful Kunwar, Jagipatti, Pursawna, Benipur, Sarairajshah, Brahimpur, Mengalpur, Darkha Sunderpur, Sonpur Mankanth, Darakha, Sunderpur, Loharata, Haripur, Jangal Tikari, Jangal Ramnagar, Raipurfulwari, Mahmudpur, Sarairajshah, Pursawna and Benipur, at intermediate level (6.01-9.00%) in Muhammadpur, Rajpur Kohra, Himmatgarh, Purabgaon, Gaderi, Pirthipur, Korarigirdharshah, Sunderpur, Nawanwa, Wartarampur, Chachakapur, Kherauna, Bhaganpur, Walipur, Naugawna, Bhupatpur and Laukipur, and at low level (3.01-6.00%) in Nainaha, Wahapur, Ramdaipur and Tala villages. Very low percentage (<3.00%) of total wastelands is seen in Trilokpur situated in the northern part of the block. The pattern of village level distribution of wastelands indicates that these lands are not concentrated in any part of the block. In many villages, their proportion is high due to environmental and anthropogenic reasons.

2.5 Conclusion

The wastelands are lands which are uncultivable or have been left uncultivated due to different constraints, but had been cultivated previously. The wastelands of Amethi Block are classified into six types : waterlogged land, usar land, banjar land, old fallow land, fallow land and other types of wasteland. The area of wastelands in Sultanpur District formed 14.18% of its total area in 1986-87. It was 9.71% in the case of Amethi Block. There was 9.92% increase in this area from 1977-78 to 1981-82 and 4.18% from 1981-82 to

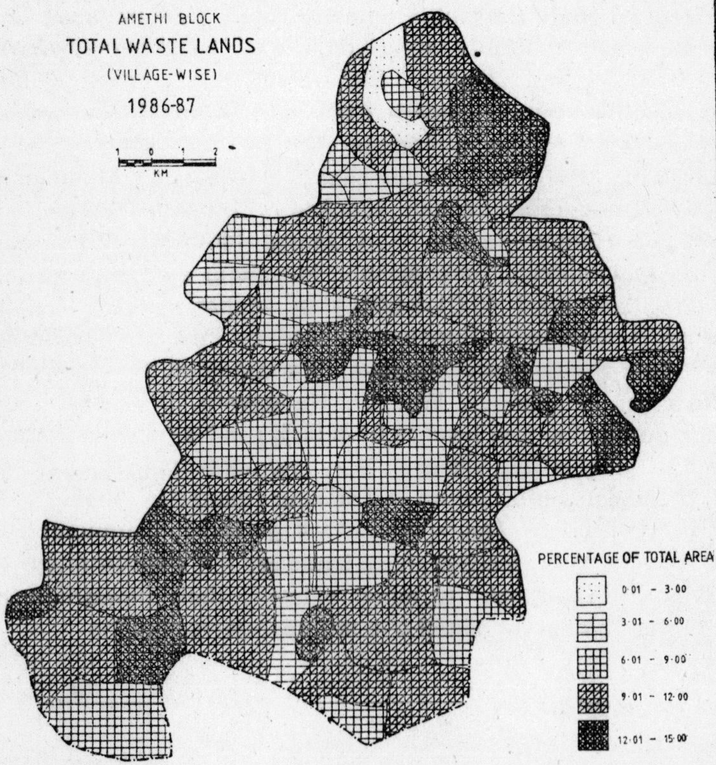

AMETHI BLOCK
TOTAL WASTE LANDS
(VILLAGE-WISE)
1986-87
1 0 1 2
KM
PERCENTAGE OF TOTAL AREA
0·01 - 3·00
3·01 - 6·00
6·01 - 9·00
9·01 - 12·00
12·01 - 15·00

MAP - 9

1986-87. The fall in their growth has been due to the fact that most of the wastelands have begun to be utilized for some purpose or the other, specially for afforestation and construction activities. Relatively high proportion of water-logged land has been found in Naraini and Katara Hulasi villages, while in most other villages of the block, their proportion is very low. Very high proportion of usar land has been found in village Trilokpur, of banjar land in Dehra, Kudwa Mahmudpur Naraini, Dhandhudhar, Sunderpur, Loniapur, Raipurfulwari, Mahmuddpur and Trilokpur, of old fallow land in Saraikhema and Ramnagar Mafi, and of other types of wasteland in Tikari. Very high proportion of total wastelands is seen in Saraiya Duhan, Dalshalpur. Biyasiya, Maharajpur, Baratali, Dhandhudhar, Dedhpasar. Hathkila, Bharathipur, Loniapur, Katarahimmatsingh, Umapurgangapatti, Persauli, Ramnagarmafi, Manafnagar and Sarai Khema and very low proportion in Teri.

Reference

1. Stamp L.D. *Land of Britain : Its Use and Misuse*, Vol. XV No. V. 1968, AMU G.S. Aligarh.

3

Determinants of Wasteland Formation

3.1 Introduction

The spatial distribution and the marked growth in the area of wastelands in Sultanpur District and Amethi Block necessitate probe into the cause and effect phenomenon of wastelands. The causative factors responsible for the development of wastelands are numerous, but the predominant ones can be identified and understood easily.

Formation of wastelands as a type of land form can be attributed to complex processes interacting at varying levels. Thus, it was considered necessary to investigate the factors affecting wastelands of Amethi Block at village level. It is assumed that the development of wastelands occurs through unhealthy interaction of a triangle of agencies—man, nature and technology. In other words, when the environment is severe, man's ability to interact with nature to his advantage is curtailed and he fails to fully avail himself of the land resources. On the other hand, when the technology is very low, wastelands spread. On the whole, the combined impact of interaction between man and nature and varying levels of technological inputs are considered to be the main factors involved in the formation of wastelands. Though the natural factors assume primary importance, man's varying levels of ability to utilize land through technological innovations also accelerate wasteland formation. Therefore, it is necessary to clearly identify and investigate all determinants of wasteland formation.

Based on the above assumptions, various natural (morphometric, hydrologic, pedogenic) and anthropogenic factors were selected for analysing each wasteland type separately, because generalisation cannot be made for all the wasteland types taken together for the reason that different factors have varying impacts on them. The major determinants have been grouped under two main heads and subdivided as follows:

(A) Natural determinants
- (a) Morphometric
  1. Slope
  2. Ruggedness number
- (b) Hydrologic
  3. Drainage density
  4. Quality of water (pH)
  5. Behaviour of water table
- (c) Pedogenic
  6. NPK of the soil
  7. pH of the soil

(B) Anthropogenic determinant
  8. Land concentration (Gini's coefficient)

3.2 Determinants in Wasteland

(1) Slope

The average slope in Amethi Block at village level varies from one village to another (Map 10). The slope is high (1.61°-2.00° in Kohra, Jarimpur Naraini, Sarwanpur and Bhushari, intermediate (1.21°-1.60°) in Kakwa, Gaderi, Ramgarh, Hathkila, Chachhakapur and Haripur, low (0.81-1.20%) in Dalshahpur, Saidpur, Saraiyaduban, Dehra, Maharajpur, Loharata Ramdaipur, Jangalramnagar Laukipur, Loniapur, Himmatgarh and Dedhpasar, and very low (0.80%) in the rest of the villages. In the last category, the village land is almost flat.

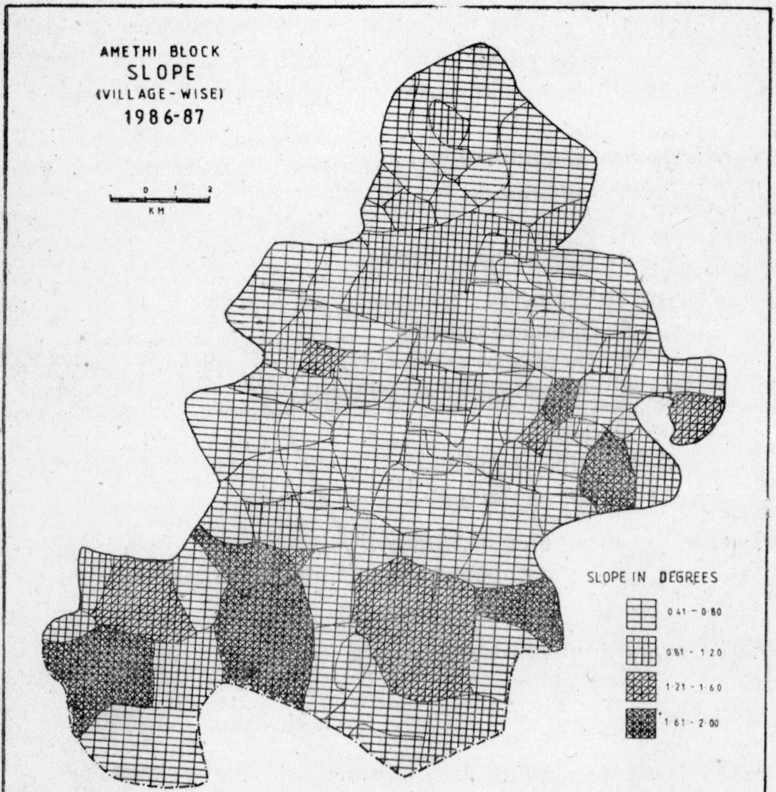
AMETHI BLOCK
SLOPE
(VILLAGE-WISE)
1986-87
0 1 2
KM
SLOPE IN DEGREES
0·41 – 0·80
0·81 – 1·20
1·21 – 1·60
1·61 – 2·00
MAP 10

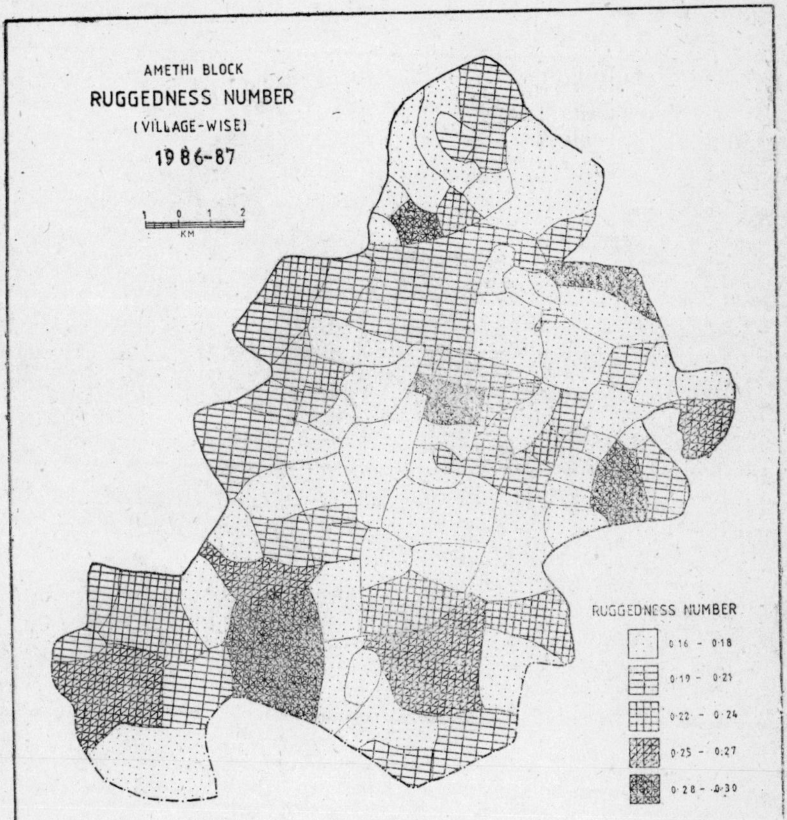
AMETHI BLOCK
RUGGEDNESS NUMBER
(VILLAGE-WISE)
1986-87
1 0 1 2
KM
RUGGEDNESS NUMBER
0·16 - 0·18
0·19 - 0·21
0·22 - 0·24
0·25 - 0·27
0·28 - 0·30

MAP – 11

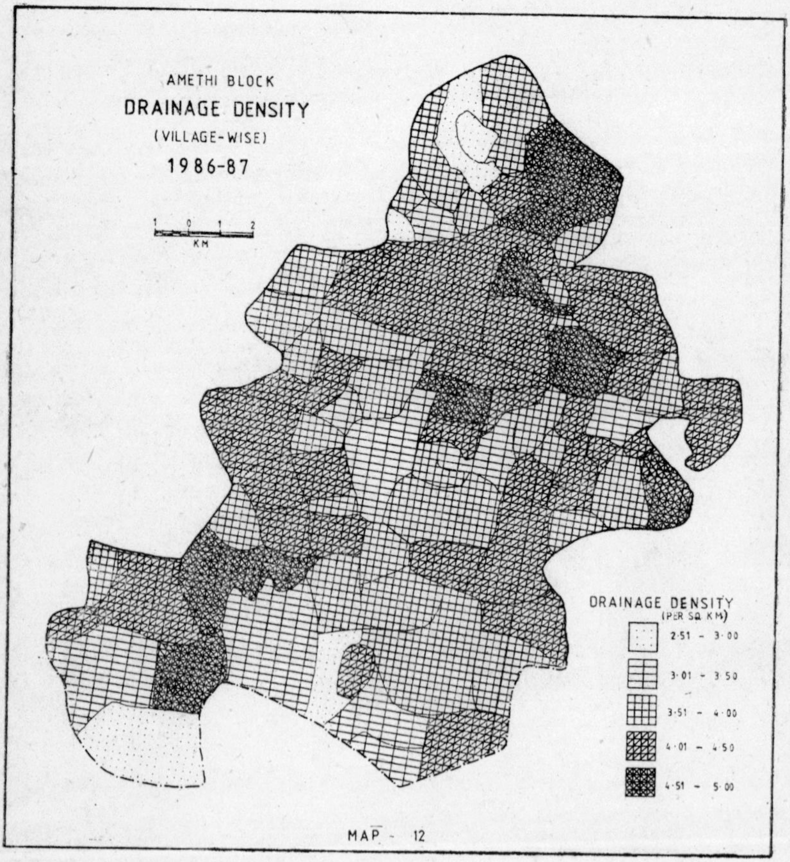
AMETHI BLOCK
DRAINAGE DENSITY
(VILLAGE-WISE)
1986-87
1 0 1 2
KM
DRAINAGE DENSITY
(PER SQ KM)
2·51 - 3·00
3·01 - 3·50
3·51 - 4·00
4·01 - 4·50
4·51 - 5·00

MAP - 12

(2) Ruggedness number

Village-wise ruggedness number values are given in Map 11. Very high ruggedness number (0.28-0.30) is observed in Naraini, Ramdaipur. Loniapur and Jairampur, high (0.25-0.27) in Kohara, Ramgarh, Maharajpur and Hathkila, intermediate (0.22-0.24) in Kakawa, Bhushari, Gaderi, Haripur, Bhaganpur and Chachakapur, low (0.19-0.20) in Dalshahpur, Saidpur, Saraiyaduban, Maharajpur, Sultanpur, Rajpur Kohra, Dehra, Dedhasar, Wariarampur, Ramdevpur, Darakh, Sonpurmankanth, Loharata, Tala, Jangaltikari, Jangalramnagar, Basudevpur and Persauli and very low (<0.18) in the rest of the villages of the block.

(3) Drainage density

Computed artificial and natural drainage density values are depicted in Map 12. Very high drainage density (4.51-5.00 per sq km) is seen in Saraiyaduban, Biyasiya, Saraikhema, Maharajpur, Loniapur, Dedhpasar, Sarairajshah, Ramnagar Mafi, Baratali, Dehra, Bhushahari, Gangauli, Gyanchandpur, Rebha Sarwanpur, Bherathipur, Sultanpur, Maharajpur, Sonpur Mankanth, Mochewa, Darakha, Sunderpur, Katara Hulsi, Jangal Tikari, Jangalramnagar, Raipurfulwari, Mahmudpur, Jagiputti, Hathkila, Persauli, Pursawna and Bhupatpur, intermediate (3.51-4.00) in Saidpur, Agahar, Sunderpur, Tala, Bhaganpur, Kushithali, Loharta, Himmatgarh, Ramgarh, Gaderi, Purabgaon, Pirthipur, Jairam, Mahso, Katara, Fulkunwar, Basuwapur, Katara Maharani Trilokpur, Wahapur and Bhupatpur, low (3.01-3.50) in Khara, Naraini, Kudwamadpur, Rajpurkohra, Nuwanwa, Wariarampur, Kherauna, and Haripur villages and very low (<3.00) in Muhammadpur, Nainaha, Wahapur, Laukipur and Teri.

(4) Quality of water (pH)

Quality of water as indicated by its pH value (Map 13) is very high (8.71-9.00) in Sarairajshah. Ramnagar Mafi, Marafanagar and Dedhpasar, high (8.41 – 8.70) in Dandupur,

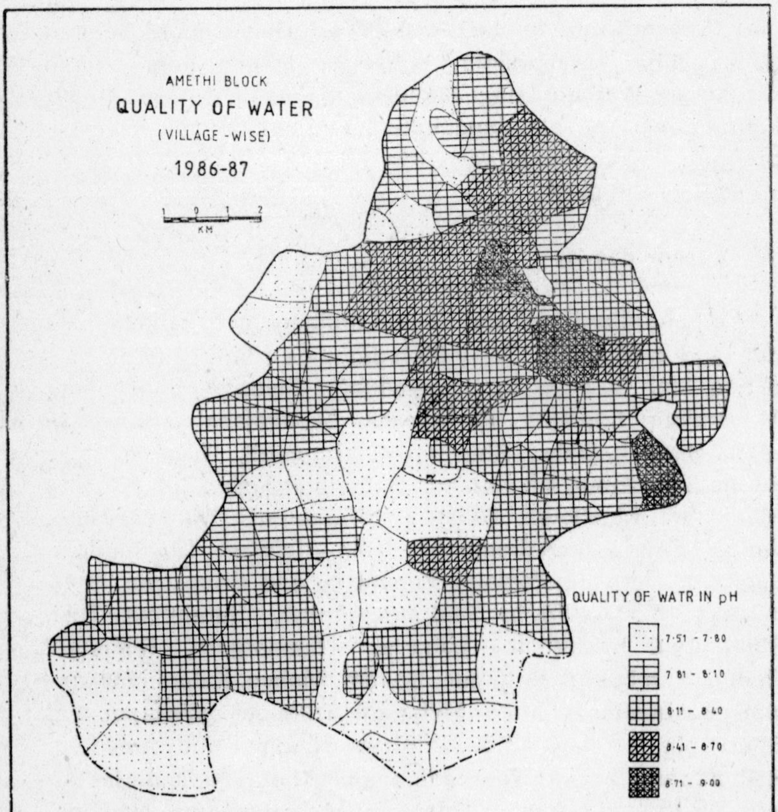
AMETHI BLOCK
QUALITY OF WATER
(VILLAGE-WISE)
1986-87
1 0 1 2
KM
QUALITY OF WATR IN pH
7·51 - 7·80
7·81 - 8·10
8·11 - 8·40
8·41 - 8·70
8·71 - 9·00

MAP - 13

Saraikhema and Persauli, intermediate (8.11-8.40) in Saraiyaduban, Naraini, Kakwa, Biyasiya, Maharajpur, Darkha, Bhushahari, Gangauli Ramdevpur, Wariarampur and Benipur, low (7.81-8 10) in Agahar, Maharajpur Sultanpur, Mahaso, Jairampur, Jamalpatti, Brahimpur, Chachakapur, Sunderpur, Katara Hulsi, Haripur, Nauganwna Trilokpur, Bhupatpur, Laukipur and Katara Maharani, and very low in Kohara, Muhammadpur. Nainaha, Kudwa Mahmudpur, Purabgaon, Gaderi, Prithipur, Himmatgarh, Dehra, Korarigirdhanshah, Mangalpur, Nauganwa Saraithiramati Mochwa Jhaunei, Tala, Bhaganpur, Wahpur, Ramdaipur, Walipur and Teri.

(5) Behaviour of water table

Water table in the block is normal (<25 ft). It is seen from Map 14 that the water table is very high (23-25 ft) in Dedhpasar, Katara Himmatsingh, Loniapur, Marafanagar, Baratali, Maharajpur and Saraiya Dubam, high (20-22 ft) in Saidpur, Kakwan Dalshahpur, Maharajpur, Sultanpur, Dhandhu Dhar, Umpaurganapatti, Hathkila, Saraikhema, Dandupur, Ramnagar Mafi Kohra, Naraini, Biyasiya, Purabgaon, Ramgarh, Korarigirdhar Shah, Mangolpur. Mochwa, Jhaunei, Sunderpur, Sonpurmankanth, Loharata, Jairampur, Mahaso, Jagipatti, Kataraful Kunwar, Kherauna, Jangaltikari, Raipurfulwari, Basuopur and Trilokpur, low (14-16 ft) in Muhammadpur, Dehra, Prithipur, Gaderi, Agahar, Saraihirmati, Darakha, Bhaganpur, Jangal Tikari, Kushithali and Katara Maharani and very low (<13 ft) in Laukipur, Teri, Naugawana, Wahapur, Tala, Nawanwa, Katara Hulasi, Nainaha, Kudwamdhammadpur Rajpur Kohara, Bhushahari and Himmatgarh.

(6) NPK of the soil

The average NPK value of the soil in the villages of the block is marginal (<3.25%), which shows that the fertility status of the soil in the area for producing crops or for the survival of plants is very poor (Map 15). It is high in Teri, Katara Maharani, Muhammadpur, Nainaha, Wariarampur, Katara Hulasi, Kherauna, Jangalramnagar, Benipur, Basuwapu

AMETHI BLOCK
BEHAVIOUR OF WATER TABLE
VILLAGE-WISE
1986-87
1 0 1 2
KM
AVERAGE
WATER TABLE IN FEET
11 - 13
14 - 16
17 - 19
20 - 22
23 25

MAP - 14

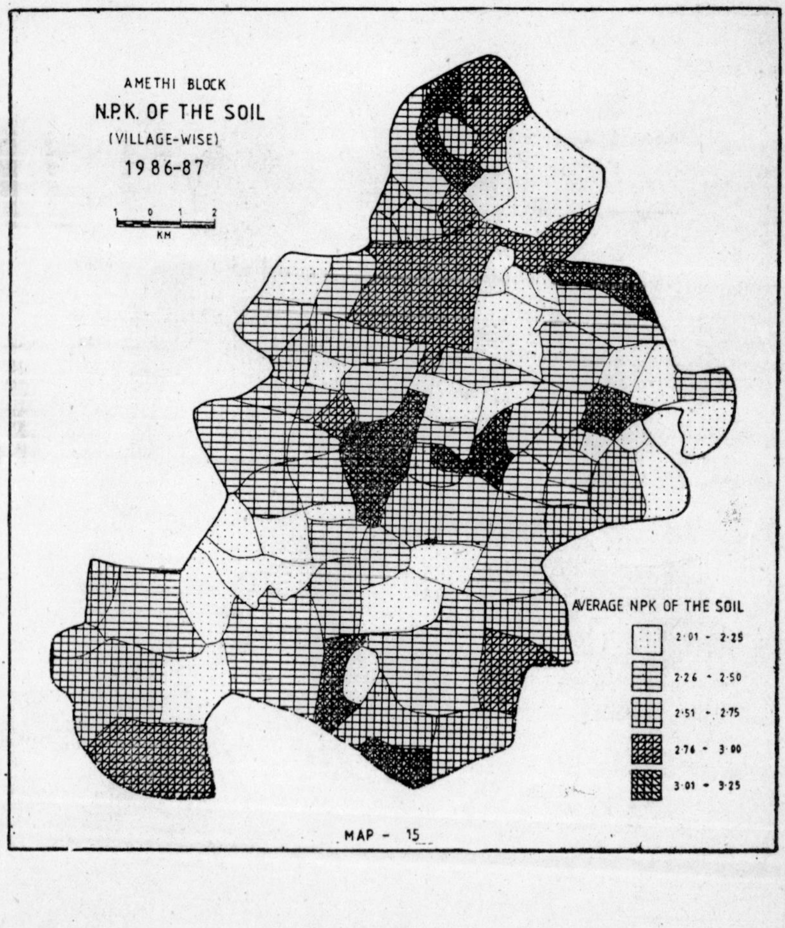

AMETHI BLOCK
N.P.K. OF THE SOIL
(VILLAGE-WISE)
1986-87
1 0 1 2
KM
AVERAGE NPK OF THE SOIL
2·01 - 2·25
2·26 - 2·50
2·51 - 2·75
2·76 - 3·00
3·01 - 3·25

MAP - 15

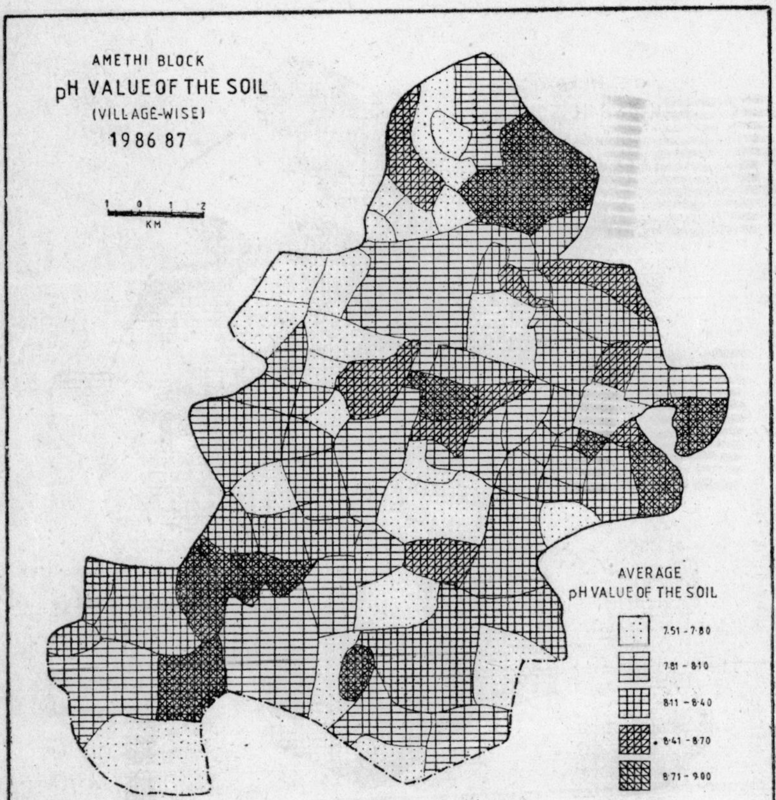
AMETHI BLOCK
pH VALUE OF THE SOIL
(VILLAGE-WISE)
1986 87
1 0 1 2
KM
AVERAGE
pH VALUE OF THE SOIL
7.51 - 7.80
7.81 - 8.10
8.11 - 8.40
8.41 - 8.70
8.71 - 9.00

MAP - 16

Table 3.1—Values of Different Variables for Soils of Wastelands in the Different Villages of Amethi Block

[Values are for 1986-87]

Sl No.	Name of village	Slope deg	Ruggedness No.	Drainage density per sq km	Quality of water (pH)	Behaviour of water table ft	NPK of soil %	pH of soil	Land conc.
(1)	(2)	(3)	(4)	(5)	(6)	(7)	(8)	(9)	(10)
1	Trilokpur	0.55	0.17	3.85	7.85	18	2.27	8.42	0.68
2	Teri	0.54	0.16	2.65	7.79	12	3.10	7.55	0.42
3	Laukipur	0.82	1.21	2.96	7.82	13	2.55	7.62	0.58
4	Katara Maharani	0.57	0.19	3.91	7.95	15	2.85	7.83	0.71
5	Sarai Khema	0.56	0.18	4.82	8.63	24	3.15	8.82	0.79
6	Dandupur	0.53	0.18	4.37	8.51	23	3.10	8.73	0.74
7	Bhupatpur	0.73	0.24	3.61	7.94	16	2.96	7.61	0.70
8	Ramdaipur	0.83	0.28	3.24	7.63	12	2.73	7.55	0.37
9	Naugawana	0.56	0.18	3.85	7.87	13	2.59	7.68	0.49
10	Wahapur	0.57	0.17	2.71	7.63	11	2.61	7.52	0.42

Contd.

Table 3.1—*Contd.*

1	2	3	4	5	6	7	8	9	10
11	Jangal Tikari	0.61	0.21	4.16	8.14	16	2.47	7.76	0.63
12	Bhaganpur	0.74	0.24	3.87	7.71	14	2.25	7.63	0.58
13	Tala	0.52	0.16	3.73	7.78	11	2.38	7.52	0.41
14	Kushi Thali	0.54	0.17	3.98	7.85	16	2.63	7.58	0.62
15	Jangal Ram Nagar	0.96	0.20	4.19	8.62	18	2.84	7.85	0.73
16	Mahmudpur	0.52	0.17	4.21	8.54	17	3.14	7.80	0.72
17	Ram Nagar Mafi	0.58	0.16	4.72	8.75	21	3.18	8.38	0.79
18	Marafapur	0.54	0.16	4.83	8.71	24	2.20	8.45	0.81
19	Wahapur	0.59	0.17	3.62	7.64	12	2.15	8.15	0.67
20	Basuwapur	0.85	0.21	3.87	7.85	17	0.85	8.32	0.69
21	Benipur	0.74	0.28	4.38	8.17	20	3.16	8.48	0.73
22	Pursawna	0.62	0.18	4.31	8.35	21	2.32	8.40	0.77
23	Ramnathpur	0.73	0.19	3.92	8.05	19	2.16	8.15	0.63
24	Sarai Rajshah	0.55	0.16	4.67	8.79	20	2.38	8.35	0.68

25	Parsauli	0.82	0.19	4.32	8.58	21	2.25	8 52	0.72
26	Katrafuikunwar	0.51	0.16	3.86	8.14	18	2.15	8.10	0.77
27	Jagi Patti	0.50	0.16	4.17	8.23	19	2.41	8.05	0.64
28	Hathkila	1.21	0.26	4.32	9.18	22	2.12	8.82	0.70
29	Jamalpatti	0.54	0.16	4.15	8.06	21	2.18	8.70	0.75
30	Kherauna	0.64	0.17	3.27	7.95	17	3.15	7.65	0.77
31	Manipur Radho	0.72	0.18	4.13	8.38	19	2.24	8.75	0.58
32	Mandharpatti	1.08	0.21	4.07	8.27	20	2.55	8.26	0.69
33	Chackakapur	1.34	0.23	3.77	7.85	16	2.45	8.15	0.62
34	Brahimpur	0.65	0.18	3.83	7.91	18	2.33	7.82	0.67
35	Sarwanpur	1.82	0.20	4.10	8.13	22	2.51	8.37	0.73
36	Katara Raja	0.74	0.19	4.43	8.68	24	2.16	8.59	0.79
37	Waria Rampur	0.70	0.19	3.14	8.26	14	3.20	7.82	0.56
38	Bharathipur	0.58	0.17	4.24	8.51	22	2.35	8.52	0.81
39	Luniapur	1.18	0.29	4.67	8.65	24	2.14	8.83	0.87
40	Raipurfulwari	0.67	0.19	4.03	8.37	18	2.48	8.35	0.73
41	Nuwanawa	0.55	0.18	3.17	7.68	13	3.10	7.82	0.54

Table 3.1—*Contd.*

(1)	(2)	(3)	(4)	(5)	(6)	(7)	(8)	(9)	(10)
42	Umappurgana-patti	0.54	0.17	3.86	7.98	21	2.32	8.65	0.77
43	Katara Hulasi	0.56	0.17	3.12	7.82	13	2.85	7.62	0.63
44	Sundarpur	0.57	0.17	3.85	8.08	19	2.35	8.25	0.67
45	Ahiraval	0.62	0.19	4.10	8.13	15	2.30	8.38	0.73
46	Haripur	0.37	0.24	4.32	7.88	13	2.18	7.75	0.52
47	Loharata	0.87	0.21	3.64	8.36	17	2.57	8.15	0.68
48	Sonpur Mankanth	0.67	0.19	4.28	8.26	19	2.45	8.38	0.62
49	Darakha	0.73	0.20	4.35	8.17	16	2.32	8.17	0.54
50	Sarai Hirmati	0.62	0.17	4.08	7.72	14	2.28	7.71	0.43
51	Aghahar	0.57	0.16	3.59	7.86	16	2.10	8.22	0.67
52	Biyasiya	0.63	0.17	4.65	8.34	19	2.08	8.75	0.79
53	Maharajpur	0.61	0.25	4.78	8.28	23	2.02	8.82	0.81
54	Chaturbhujapur	0.69	0.21	4.25	8.07	20	2.24	8.36	0.72
55	Mochwa	0.57	0.17	4.13	7.68	19	2.35	8.22	0.63
56	Jhaunei	0.72	0.20	3.85	7.63	18	2.22	8.28	0.58

57	Sultanpur	0.67	0.19	4.07	7.89	21	2.41	8.39	0.66
58	Purabgaon	0.61	0.18	3.73	7.72	17	2.30	7.81	0.53
59	Pirthipur	0.53	0.16	3.81	7.77	16	2.35	7.88	0.56
60	Gaderi	1.54	0.24	3.89	7.69	15	2.25	7.62	0.51
61	Dhandhudhar	0.58	0.16	4.27	8.54	21	2.15	8.42	0.73
62	Korari Girdharshah	0.57	0.17	3.64	7.68	17	2.86	7.67	0.59
63	Mangalpur	0.54	0.16	3.77	7.79	18	2.51	7.72	0.64
64	Gangauli	0.52	0.16	4.12	8.14	20	2.43	8.14	0.71
65	Ramdevpur	0.96	0.20	4.01	8.11	21	2.35	8.22	0.72
66	Rebha	0.52	0.16	4.28	8.23	21	2.28	8.36	0.78
67	Gyanchandpur	0.59	0.16	4.13	8.20	19	2.38	8.27	0.69
68	Mahaso	0.58	0.17	3.71	7.91	17	2.85	7.75	0.58
69	Jairampur	1.88	0.29	3.94	7.86	19	2.65	8.11	0.53
70	Dedhpasar	0.91	0.19	4.72	8.72	24	2.12	8.82	0.82
71	Bhusahari	1.79	0.23	4.14	8.19	13	2.67	8.18	0.73
72	Himmatgarh	0.54	0.16	2.62	7.68	12	2.82	7.71	0.59
73	Dehra	0.92	0.19	4.16	7.72	14	2.73	7.83	0.63

Table 3.1—*Contd.*

1	2	3	4	5	6	7	8	9	10
74	Rajapurkohara	0.73	0.19	3.21	7.68	13	3.15	7.55	0.52
75	Kudwa Mahmudpur	0.58	0.17	3.12	7.73	13	2.86	7.86	0.62
76	Ramgarh	1.36	0.26	3.85	8.16	18	2.32	8.35	0.68
77	Baratali	0.52	0.16	4.17	8.38	22	2.21	8.42	0.73
78	Nainaha	0.59	0.17	2.78	7.68	12	3.22	7.51	0.54
79	Naraini	1.92	1.29	3.18	8.15	19	2.35	7.99	0.67
80	Saraiya Duban	0.86	0.21	4.54	8.74	23	2.12	8.78	0.82
81	Muhammadpur	0.62	0.18	2.96	7.67	15	2.85	7.68	0.66
82	Kohara	1.63	0.25	3.13	7.77	18	2.62	7.98	0.72
83	Kakwa	1.41	0.24	4.08	8.33	21	2.45	8.23	0.78
84	Saidpur	0.92	0.21	3.83	8.16	20	2.67	8.12	0.71
85	Dalshahpur	0.87	0.20	4.16	8.31	22	2.45	8.36	0.79

and Bhupatpur and very low (<2.25%) in Saraiyaduban. Biyasiya, Maharajpur, Agahar, Jhaunei, Gaderi, Dhandhudhar, Loniapur, Katara Himmat Singh. Dhedhpasar, Jamalpatti, Hathkila, Katara Fulkunwar, Persauli, Mahmudpur, Ramnagar Mafi, Haripur, Bhaganpur, Saraichema and Dandupur.

(7) pH of the soil

The average pH of soil in the block at village level varies from 7.51 to 9.00 (Map 16). High pH of soil is observed in Saraiyaduban, Biyasiya, Maharajpur, Barathali, Dhandhudhar. Dedhpasar, Hathkila, Jamalpatti, Katarahimmatsingh, Bharathipur, Umapur Ganapatti, Persauli, Benipur, Marafanagar, Saraikheme, Dandupur and Trilokpur and very low (<7.81) in Muhammadpur, Rajpur Kohara, Nainaha, Gaderi, Himmatgarh, Mahaso, Korarigirdhar Shah, Mangolpur, Mochwa, Bhaganpur, Tala, Jangal Tikari, Katara Hulasi, Mahmudpur, Dherauna, Laukipur, Teri, Naugawa, Wahapur, Ramdaipur and Bhupatpur.

(8) Land concentration

Land concentration (Gini's coefficient) is very high (0.79-0.90) in Dalshahpur, Saraiya Duban, Biyasia Maharajpur, Dedhpusar, Katarahimmat Singh, Loniapur, Bharathipur, Ramnagar Mafi, Marafanagar and Saraikhema, high (0.67-0.78) in Kohra, Kakwa, Saidpur, Naraini Aghar, Maharajpur, Bartali, Ramgarh, Bhushahari, Gangauli, Dandhudhar, Ramdevpur, Rebha, Hathkila, Kherauna, Sarwanpur, Brahimpur, Kataraful Kunwar, Sarairajshah, Mohamudpur Purswana, Benipur, Walipuri, Umapurganapattai, Sonpur mankanth and Katarhulsi, intermediate (0.55-0.66) in Muhammadpur, Kudwamahmudpur, Dehra, Himmatgarh, Pirthipur, Sultanpur, Jhaunei, Mochwa, Korarigirdharshah, Wariarampur, Mangalpur, Mahso, Loharata, Haripur, Kushithali, Jangaltikari, Jangal Ramnagar, Bhaganpur and Laukipur, low (0.43-0.54) in Rajpur Kohra, Nainaha, Gaderi, Purabgaon, Jairampur, Nauwanawa, Saraihimati, Darakha villages and very low (<0.42) in Tala, Wahapur, Ramdaipur and Teri.

3.3 Analysis of the Correlation Matrix and Stepwise Regression

The correlation matrix was prepared to see the trend of correlation among different independent variables for various types of wastelands. Stepwise regression analysis was done to see as to how the parameters change when new variables are added one by one.

Correlation matrix data given in (Table 3.2) indicate that there is significant positive correlation between drainage density (X_3) (independent variable) and the proportion of waterlogged land (Y) (dependent variable). which is significant at 1% level of significance, because high drainage density helps in accumulation of surface water in depressed areas, which is helpful in the rise of water table.

There is positive correlation between slope (X_1) and ruggedness number (X_2), which is significant at 5% and 10% levels of significance respectively. High values of slope and ruggedness number provide positive conditions for greater surface water flow and accumulation of water in low-lying areas. Behaviour of water table (X_5) has positive correlation with the proportion of waterlogged land, but it is significant at 5% level of significance. There is negative correlation between the NPK of the soil, which is significant at 10% level of significance, because low NPK of soil means low fertility status. The other variables, viz. pH of the soil (X_8), land concentration (X_7) and quality of water as represented by pH (X_4) have positive correlations with the waterlogged land, but this relationship is insignificant. Therefore, these variables fail to provide explanation for variation in the proportion of waterlogged land at village level in Amethi Block.

The stepwise analysis was done to study the correlation of different dependent variables with the proportion of waterlogged land as the independent variable. The land intercorrelation matrix obtained is given in (Table 3.3). The most dominant variable in explaining the variability in waterlogged land is seen to be the slope (X_1), which explains 29.9% variation in waterlogged land at village level in the block. It is interesting to note that in the subsequent step, the variable

Table 3.2—Correlation Matrix for Waterlogged Land

Symbol	Variable	Y	X_1	X_2	X_3	X_4	X_5	X_6	X_7	X_8
Y	% of waterlogged land	1.000								
X_1	Slope, deg	0.548**	1.000							
X_2	Ruggedness No.	0.317*	0.247	1.000						
X_3	Drainage density per sq km	0.639***	0.053	−0.199	1.000					
X_4	Quality of water (pH)	0.152	0.072	−0.064	0.697***	1.000				
X_5	Behaviour of water table	0.421**	0.126	−0.120	0.721***	0.734***	1.000			
X_6	NPK of soil, %	−0.343*	0.144	−0.014	0.514**	−0.364*	−0.435*	1.000		
X_7	Land conc.	0.136	0.101	−0.120	0.720***	0.703***	0.825***	0.522**	1.000	
X_8	pH of soil	0.243	0.076	−0.083	0.597***	0.670***	0.776***	−0.305*	0.714***	1.000

*** Significant at 1% level of significance

** Significant at 5% level of significance

* Significant at 10% level of significance

Table 3.3—Stepwise Regression Analysis of Waterlogged Land

Variables		Intercept	Regression coeff.	*SE*	*T*	R^2	Increase	*R*	R^2	*F*
Step 1)	(1	0.092632	0.635	0.107	5.96***	0.299	—	0.547	0.291	35.55***
Step 2)	(3	0.255998	0.607	0.106	5.72***	0.327	0.028	0.572	0.311	19.98***

***Significant at 1% level of significance.

Table 3.4—Correlation Matrix for Usar Land

Symbol	Variable	Y	X_1	X_2	X_3	X_4	X_5	X_6	X_7	X_8
Y	% of usar land	1.000								
X_1	Slope, deg	0.295	1.000							
X_2	Ruggedness No.	0.168	0.247	1.000						
X_3	Drainage density per sq km	0.208	0.053	−0.699	1.000					
X_4	Quality of water (pH)	0.191	0.072	−0.064	0.697***	1.000				

X_5 Behaviour of water table	0.317*	0.126	-0.120	0.721***	0.734***	1.000		
X_6 NPK of soil	-0.385*	-0.144	-0.014	-0.514*	-0.364*	-0.435*	1.000	
X_7 pH of soil	0.762***	-0.101	-0.120	0.720***	0.703***	0.825***	-0.522**	1.000
X_8 Land conc	0.478**	0.076	-0.083	0.597**	0.670***	0.776***	-0.305*	0.714*** 1.000

*** Significant at 1% level of significance

** Significant at 5% level of significance

* Significant at 10% level of significance.

Table 3.5—Stepwise Regression Analysis of Usar Land

Variables		Intercept	Regression coeff.	*SE*	*T*	R^2	Increase in R^2	*R*	R^2	*F*
Step 1)	(7	2.413898	1.107	0.296	3.73***	0.144	—	0.379	0.134	13.95***
Step 2)	(8	2.388459	2.187	1.013	2.16	0.189	0.045	0.436	0.170	9.61***
			1.183	0.292	4.05***					

*** Significant at 1% level of significance.

Table 3.6—Correlation Matrix for Banjar Land

Symbol	Variable	Y	X_1	X_2	X_3	X_4	X_5	X_6	X_7	X_8
Y	% of banjar land	1.000								
X_1	Slope, deg	−0.089	1.000							
X_2	Ruggedness No.	−0.168	0.247	1.000						
X_3	Drainage density	0.352*	0.053	−0.199	1.000					
X_4	Quality of water (pH)	0.429*	0.072	−0.064	0.697***	1.000				
X_5	Behaviour of water table	0.215	0.126	−0.120	0.721***	0.734***	1.000			
X_6	NPK of soil	0.346*	−0.144	−0.014	−0.514**	−0.364*	−0.435	1.000		
X_7	pH of soil	0.623**	−0.101	−0.120	0.720	0.703***	0.825***	−0.522**	1.000	
X_8	Land conc.	0.403*	0.076	−0.083	0.597**	0.670***	0.776***	−0.395*	0.714***	1.000

*** Significant at 1% level of significance

*£ Significant at 5% level of significance

* Significant at 10% level of significance.

drainage density (X_3) enters and jointly with variable X_1 explains 32.7% total variation in the proportion of waterlogged land.

Other variables could not enter in the stepwise regression analysis, indicating that these variables fail to explain the variation in the proportion of waterlogged land in the Block at village level.

(2) Usar Land

There is positive correlation between usar land and pH of the soil (X_7), which is significant at 1% level of significance, indicating that the villages having proportionately high percentage of usar land have high pH of the soil; because of excessive concentration of neutral salts, mainly chlorides and sulphates of sodium in usar soils, the pH of the soil is high (Table 3.4). There is positive correlation between land concentration and the proportion of usar land, which is significant at 5% level of significance, because farmers with large land holdings are unable to regenerate its fertility status, while their involvement is more in fertile soils from which they are sure to get good returns. The behaviour ot water table (X_5) has positive correlation with the proportion of usar land, which is significant at 10% level of significance. In usar areas, water table is low and at a certain stratum the solid profile is not very permeable due to the presence of Kankar pan. As a result of this, water table rises and water gets enriched in soluble salts. There is negative correlation between the NPK of soil and the proportion of usar land, but this relationship is not strong, being significant at 10% level of significance. The other variables, viz. slope (X_1), ruggedness number (X_2), drainage density (X_3), and quality of water (X_4), have positive correlation with the proportion of usar land. But these variables fail to explain the variation in the proportion of usar land, because their relationship is insignificant.

The values of different independent variables (X) for usar lands indicate a high degree of multicollinearity among them. To remove inconsistencies arising from this multicollinearity, stepwise regression analysis was attempted. In this exercise percentage of usar land is considered as the dependent variable (Y) and other natural and anthropogenic factors as independent variables (X). The intercorrelation matrix obtained from stepwise regression analysis is given in (Table 3.5). The most dominant variable in stepwise regression in explaining the variability of usar land is the pH value of the soil (X_8). It indicates 14.4% variation in the proportion of usar land. In the subsequent step, variable X_7 enters and jointly with variable X_8 explains 18.9% total variation in the proportion of usar land at village level. But other variables could not enter in this stepwise regression, indicating that there are other factors than these variables which are responsible for the proportion of usar land. Thus, among the selected variables, pH of the soil and land concentration are the important variables in explaining the variation in the proportion of usar land.

(3) Banjar Land

There is positive correlation between the percentage of banjar land and pH of the soil (X_8), which is significant at 1% level of significance (Table 3.6). Soils with high pH have high concentrations of salts, which hamper crop production. The variables X_7 (land concentration), X_4 (quality of water) and X_3 (drainage density) have positive correlations with the proportion of banjar land. These variables are not of much importance here, because their correlation with the Y variable (banjar land) is significant at 10% level of significance. There is negative correlation between the NPK of soil and the proportion of banjar land, which is significant at 10% level of significance. There is positive corelation between the behaviour of the water table (X_5) and the proportion of banjar land, but this relationship is insignificant. Slope (X_1) and ruggedness number (X_2) have negative correlations with the proportion of banjar land.

The correlation matrix for various independent and dependent variables shows positive correlations of some of the variables with the proportion of banjar land. Stepwise regression analysis was attempted to see as to how many of these variables can explain the variation in the proportion of banjar land (Table 3.7). The variable X_8 (pH of soil) is found to be a dominant variable in explaining the variation in the proportion of banjar land. It indicates 24.9% variation. Other environmental and anthropogenic factors could not enter in the stepwise regression analysis, indicating that they fail to explain the variation in the proportion of banjar land.

(4) Old Fallow Land

There is positive correlation between pH of the soil (X_8), land concentration (X_7) and the proportion of old fallow land, which is significant at 10% level of significance (Table 3.8). Slope (X_1), ruggedness number (X_2), drainage density (X_3), quality of water (X_4) and behaviour of water table (X_5) have insignificant relationship with the percentage of old fallow land.

The correlation matrix indicates multi-collinearity among the independent variables. To remove the resulting inconsistencies, stepwise regression analysis was done (Table 3.9). In the first step of this analysis, variable X_8 (pH of the soil) enters; it explains 11.3% variation in the proportion of old fallow land. Other variables do not get incorporated, indicating that the other natural and anthropogenic variables are incapable of explaining the variation in the proportion of old fallow land. Some other factors are responsible for the uneven distribution of old fallow land.

(5) Fallow Land

A significant positive correlation is seen between the drainage density (X_3) and percentage of fallow land. The relationship between these variables is significant at 5% level of significance. Variable X_4 (quality of water as represented by pH) has positive correlation with the proportion of fallow land and it is significant at 5% level of significance (Table 3.10). The behaviour of water table has a positive correlation with the proportion of fallow land, which is significant at 10% level of significance. The relationship between

Table 3.7—Stepwise Regression Analysis of Banjar Land

Variables	Intercept	Regression coeff	*SE*	*T*	R^2	Increase in R^2	*R*	R^2	*F*
Step 1) (7	2.009181	0.913	0.247	2.08***	0.239	—	0.323	0.646	14.3

*** Significant at 1% level of significance.

Table 3.8—Correlation Matrix Old Fallow Land

Symbol	Variables	Y	X_1	X_2	X_3	X_4	X_5	X_6	X_7	X_8
Y	% of old fallow land	1.000								
X_1	Slope, deg	0.176	1.000							
X_2	Ruggedness No.	-0.045	0.247	1.000						
X_3	Drainage density	0.286	0.053	-0.199	1.000					
X_4	Quality of water (pH)	0.294	0.092	-0.064	0.697***	1.000				
X_5	Behaviour of water table	0.246	0.126	-0.120	0.721	0.734***	1.000			

X_6 NPK of soil	−0.375*	−0.144	−0.014**	−0.514*	−0.364	−0.435*	1.000		
X_7 pH of soil	0.436*	−0.101	−0.120	0.720***	0.703***	0.825***	−0.522**	1.000	
X_8 Land conc.	0.425*	0.076	−0.083	0.0597**	0.670***	0.776***	−0.305*	0.7147***	1.000

*** Significant at 1% level of significance

** Significant at 5% level of significance

* Significant at 10% level of significance.

Table 3.9—Stepwise Regression Analysis of Old Fallow Land

Variables	Intercept	Regression coeff.	SE	T	R^2	Increase in R^2	R	R^2	F
Step 1) (7	2.296997	0.917	0.282	3.25***	0.113	—	0.336	0.102	10.5***

*** Significant at 1% level of significance.

Table 3.10—Correlation Matrix for Fallow Land

Symbol	Variable	Y	X_1	X_2	X_3	X_4	X_5	X_6	X_7	X_8
Y	% of fallow land	1.000								
X_1	Slope, deg	-0.160	1.000							
X_2	Ruggedness No.	-0.176	0.247	1.000						
X_3	Drainage density	0.544**	0.053	-0.199	1.000					
X_4	Quality of water (pH)	0.479**	0.072	-0.064	0.697***	1.000				
X_5	Behaviour of water table	0.427*	0.126	-0.120	0.721***	0.734***	1.000			
X_6	NPK of soil	-0.372*	-0.144	-0.014	-0.514***	-0.364	-0.435	1.000		
X_7	pH of soil	0.418	-0.101	-0.120	0.720	0.703	0.825	-0.522	1.000	
X_8	Land conc.	0.382	0.076	-0.083	0.597	0.670	0.776	-0.305	0.714	1.000

*** Significant at 1% level of significance.

** Significant at 5% level of significance.

* Significant at 10% level of significance.

the variable X_6 (NPK of the soil) and the proportion of fallow land is negative, being significant at 10% level of significance. There is positive correlation of pH of the soil and land concentration with the percentage of fallow land. These relationships are not of much importance, because they are significant only at 10% level of significance. Slope and ruggedness number have negative correlations with the proportion of fallow land.

The results of stepwise regression analysis done taking the proportion of fallow land as dependent variable (Y) and other environmental and anthropogenic factors as independent variables (X) are given in (Table 3.11). Stepwise regression analysis shows that in the first step, variable X_4 (quality of water) enters and explains 22.9% variation in the proportion of fallow land. In the second step, variable X_3 (drainage density) jointly with variable X_4 explains 25.3% total variation in the proportion of fallow land. The other variables do not get incorporated in stepwise regression analysis, indicating that they cannot explain the variation in the proportion of fallow land at village level.

(6) Other Types of Wastelands

There is positive correlation between NPK of the soil and the proportion of other types of wasteland, which is significant at 10% level of significance (Table 3.12). Variable X_8 (land concentration) has a significant positive correlation with the proportion of other types of wasteland, being significant at 10% level of significance. Farmers with large land holdings do not pay much attention to the improvement of such lands, as they have other good quality land from which they are sure of getting good returns. With limited input, they are unable to cultivate all land. The other variables, viz., slope (X_1), ruggedness number (X_2), drainage density (X_3), quality of water (X_4), behaviour of water table (X_5) and pH of the soil (X_7) have not much importance in explaining the relationship with the proportion of other types of wasteland, because their correlations are insignificant. The system of explaining with endogenic variables discussed above shows the exist-

Table 3.11—Stepwise Regression Analysis of Fallow Land

Variables		Intercept	Regression coeff.	*SE*	*T*	R^2	Increase in R^2	*R*	R^2	*F*
Step 1)	(4	4.292062	2.630	0.529	4.97***	0.229	—	0.479	0.219	24.67***
Step 2)	(3	6.266952	0.839	0.519	1.62***	0.253	0.034	0.503	0.235	13.88***
			1.807	0.731	2.47***					

*** Significant at 1% level of significance.

Table 3.12—Correlation Matrix for Other Types of Wastelands

Symbol	Variables	Y	X_1	X_2	X_3	X_4	X_5	X_6	X_7	X_8
Y	% of other types of wastelands	1.000								
X_1	Slope, deg.	−0.023	1.000							
X_2	Ruggedness No.	−0.067	0.247	1.000						
X_3	Drainage density	0.212	0.053	−0.199	1.000					
X_4	Quality of water (pH)	0.123	0.072	−0.064	0.697***	1.000				

X_5 Behaviour of water table	0.087	0.126	0.128	−0.721***	0.734***	1.000		
X_6 NPK of soil	0.333*	−0.144	−0.014	−0.514**	−0.364*	−0.435*	1.000	
X_7 pH of soil	0.095	0.101	−0.120	0.720***	0.703***	0.825***	−0.522**	1.000
X_8 Land conc.	0.412*	0.076	−0.083	0.097**	0.670	0.776***	−0.305*	0.714***	1.000

*** Significant at 1% level of significance.
** Significant at 5% level of significance.
* Significant at 10% level of significance.

Table 3.13—Stepwise Regression Analysis of Other Types of Wastelands

Variables	Intercept	Regression coeff.	*SE*	*T*	R^2	Increase in R^2	*R*	R^2	*F*
Step 1) (8	1.025384	3.787	1.524	2.48***	0.169	—	0.263	0.058	6.17***

*** Significant at 1% level of significance.

Table 3.14—Correlation Matrix for Wastelands

Symbol	Variables	Y	X_1	X_2	X_3	X_4	X_5	X_6	X_7	X_8
Y	% of wasteland	1.000								
X_1	Slope, deg.	0.113	1.000							
X_2	Ruggedness No.	−0.095	0.247	1.000						
X_3	Drainage density	0.750***	0.053	−0.199	1.000					
X_4	Quality of water (pH)	0.741***	0.072	−0.064	0.697***	1.000				
X_5	Behaviour of water table	0.839***	0.126	−0.120	0.721***	0.734***	1.000			
X_6	NPK of soil	−0.465***	−0.144	−0.014	−0.514**	-0.364**	−0.435	1.000		
X_7	pH of soil	0.848***	0.101	−0.120	0.720***	0.703***	0.825***	−0.522**	1.000	
X_8	Land conc.	0.797***	0.076	−0.083	0.597**	0.670***	0.776***	−0.305*	0.714***	1.000

*** Significant at 1% level of significance

** Significant at 5% level of significance

* Significant at 10% level of significance.

Table 3.15—Stepwise Regression Anelysis for Wastelands

Variables		Intercept	Regression coeff.	*SE*	*T*	R^2	Increase in R^2	*R*	R^2	*F*
Step 1)	(7	3.065437	5.506	0.376	14.62***	0.720	—	0.849	0.717	213.76***
Step 2)	(8	3.928026	3.693	0.463	7.98***	0.795	0.075	0.892	0.790	159.45***
Step 3)	(3	4.537645	1.194	0.361	3.31***	0.809	0.024	0.905	0.813	122.82***
			2.803	0.513	5.46***					
			8.365	1.620	5.16*					
Step 4)	(5	5.171252	0.988	0.369	2.68***	0.828	0.009	0.910	0.819	96.51***
			0.141	0.071	2.00*					
			2.261	0.572	3.95**					
			6.763	1.782	3.79**					

*** Significant at 1% level of significance

** Significant at 5% level of significance

* Significant at 10% level of significance.

ence of a high degree of multi-collinearity among these variables.

The intercorrelation matrix obtained through stepwise regression analysis is shown in Table 3.13. The most dominant variable in the first step of regression analysis is X_8 (land concentration), which explains 16.9% variation in the proportion of other types of wasteland. The other variables could not come in the optimal regression line, indicating their failure to explain variation in the proportion of other types of wasteland.

(7) Total Wastelands

It is seen from Table 3.14 that high drainage density (X_3) causes greater soil erosion, leading to land degradation and accumulation of water in depressed areas. Thus, high drainage density is associated with high proportion of wastelands. There is positive correlation between drainage density and the proportion of wastelands, which is significant at 1% level of significance; soil with high pH has high salinity level, which causes hindrance in crop production and helps in the spread of wastelands. This is also proved statistically, since this relationship is significant at 5% level of significance.

Land concentration is seen to be high in those villages where percentage of wastelands is also high, indicating that there is positive correlation between land concentration (X_8) and the proportion of wastelands. Farmers with large sized land holdings are not interested in improving the fertility status of wastelands due to low output from them. They concentrate on good quality lands from which they are sure to get good returns. The positive correlation between wastelands and land concentration is significant at 1% level of significance. The variables slope (X_1) and ruggedness number (X_2) are not important in explaining the variation in the proportion of wastelands, because the relationship between these variables is significant.

The results of stepwise regression analysis are given in Table 3.15. It is seen that the variable X_7 (pH of the soil) enters in the first step and explains 72% variation in the proportion of wastelands. In the second step, variable X_8 (land concentration) jointly with variable X_7 explains 79.5% variation in the proportion of wastelands. In the third step, variable X_3 (drainage density) enters and explains 81.9% total variation in the proportion of wastelands jointly with variables X_7 and X_8. Lastly, in the fourth step, variable X_5 (behaviour of water table) enters, which explains 82.8% variation in the proportion of wastelands jointly with variables X_7, X_8 and X_3. Thus, the total variation in the proportion of wastelands explained by the environmental and anthropogenic factors is 82.8%. However, the interaction between the set of environmental and anthropogenic factors and the proportion of wastelands provides a clue of great significance at 1% level of significance, while the main variables explaining the percentage of wastelands are pH of the soil, land concentration, drainage density and behaviour of the water table.

3.4 Conclusion

It may be concluded that a combination of environmental and anthropogenic factors plays a major role in the spatial distribution of wastelands over various categories. Correlation matrix and stepwise regression analyses prove that drainage density and slope are the dominant variables in explaining the variation in the proportion of usar land. The main variables explaining the proportion of usar land are pH of the soil and land concentration. For banjar land and old fallow land, the dominant variable for this purpose is the pH of the soil. Quality of water (pH) and drainage density are the dominant variables in explaining the variation in the proportion of fallow land. For other types of wasteland, land concentration is the dominant variable for this purpose.

The variables that feature in explaining the variation in the proportion of total wastelands in Amethi Block are pH of the soil, land concentration, drainage density and behaviour of the water table.

4

Reclaiming Wastelands

4.1 Introduction

Soil deterioration through erosion, ultimately creating wastelands, is one of the pressing problems of the country. It has already ruined good acreage of cultivable land. If it remains unchecked, it will affect the remaining land also. In short, unless we adequately safeguard our good land, we may eventually face a serious shortage of foodgrains, fodder, fuelwood, fibre, fisheries and fruits (F^6). Hence, the conservation concept, i.e. protecting the existing cultivable land and reclaiming the already depleted wastelands figures prominently among the priority tasks of the planning agencies. Various reclamation measures have been adopted in different areas of Amethi Block covering all wasteland types, but they have not been worked on scientific lines. Some of the wasteland reclamation methods were unsuccessful after some time, because the lands reverted to their original condition due to mismanagement and the unscientific way in which the reclamation measures were adopted. In choosing wasteland reclamation methods due attention must be paid to the cost factor. The inputs and outputs must be balanced with benefits accruing from the land over the years. Time involved in reclamation is an additional factor to be considered. It has been observed that cheaper amendments are slower in reaction and give uneconomic returns in the beginning. Certain ameliorative factors, such as surplus farm commodities or industrial wastes may be available in an area, but their costs may prove prohibitive, or they may be available with difficulty at another place. Such factors have to be taken into consideration before deciding upon a particular method for reclamation of wastelands. A proper study has also to be made of the environmental and anthropogenic factors responsible for the spread of various wasteland types.

The problem of reclamation of different wasteland types cannot be considered in totality, because for different wasteland types different reclamation measures are required. Here, reclamation of three types of wastelands is discussed : (1) Easily reclaimable, (2) reclaimable with some difficulty, and (3) reclaimable with extreme difficulty. Respective measures to be adopted for their reclamation are explained. For this purpose, three villages were selected according to their capability classification. One acre wasteland of each category was subjected to various reclamation measures to see how in practice various methods work. The easily reclaimable wastelands could be reclaimed for agricultural purposes, those reclaimable with some difficulty for agroforestry and the last category, viz., reclaimable with extreme difficulty, for forestry purposes. The study was carried out during the two main cropping seasons. The various reclamation measures adopted during the reclamation of different types of wastelands are discussed below.

4.2 Reclaiming Wastelands for Agriculture

This work was done on 1 acre usar land in village Dandupur. The pH of the soil was 8.6. The reclamation measures tried were based on the package of technology worked out for the reclamation of usar land. The major components of this technology are as follows :

(a) Mechanical land levelling and bunding,

(b) Leaching,

(c) Application of a suitable chemical amendment in right quantity and proper manner as per requirement of the soil,

(d) Choice of salt tolerant crops in a proper sequence and variety,

(e) Application of fertilizer and manure in adequate quantities,

(f) Adoption of appropriate cultural and agronomic practices, and

(g) Proper utilization and management of water.

The work done in Dandupur village has revealed that for reclamation of usar lands, availability of good quality water for irrigation is an essential prerequisite. The strategy recommended for treating lands of this type includes the following measures :

(1) Proper levelling of the selected patch of land so as to obtain uniform spread of water.

(2) Making bunds along the field.

(3) Dividing the field into convenient sized plots with small earthen embankments in accordance with the slope.

(4) Making small suitable drains for the removal of excess irrigation and rain water.

(5) Leaching and flushing to flush out materials responsible for usarization.

(6) Soil testing to know the nature of the soil and to ascertain the requirement of fertilizer for getting good crop yields.

(7) Application of 40 quintals of gypsum per acre in the first season (Karif) along with 80 kg urea, 30 kg Shakti Khad, and 40 kg potash and compost.

(8) Applying 20 kg urea as top dressing.

(9) Sowing wheat in Rabi season and applying 80 kg urea, 50 kg muriate of potash and 60 kg phosphatic fertilizer per acre.

(10) Sowing easily decomposable plants (Dhaincha) before the onset of the rainy season.

(11) Mixing gypsum in powdered form with the top 10 cm of soil.

(12) Applying water after the application of gypsum in such quantity that it stands for 10-15 days prior to paddy plantation.

(13) Application of pyrite.

(14) Growing paddy in the first Kharif season.

(15) Persisting with paddy crop for a few years until a good crop is obtained.

(16) Applying nitrogen 25% in excess of the normally recommended dose without zinc application.

(17) Doing green manuring prior to sowing Rabi crop.

(18) Growing wheat crop in the Rabi season with application of 25% nitrogen in excess of the recommended dose.

(19) Sowing high yielding salt tolerant variety of wheat.

(20) Giving light but frequent irrigations in Rabi season as per requirement of the crop.

(21) Adoption of a proper crop rotation schedule for at least three years.

(22) Not leaving the land fallow for a long period.

The above discussed practices could be suitably modified to meet the requirements of a particular soil. Adequate levelling of the field, improvement of the drainage and abundant supply of good quality irrigation water are essential prerequisites for any usar land reclamation project to be taken in hand. In many cases, deterioration of the soil caused by salt is more easily rectified in comparison to reclamation of eroded land.

4.3 Reclaiming Wastelands for Agroforestry

Agroforestry involves putting land to multiple uses. Its salient purpose is to have trees and crops inter- and/or underplanted to form an integrated system of biological production within a certain area. Thus, agroforestry implies integration of trees with agricultural crops and/or livestock simultaneously or sequentially. In a broad sense, agroforestry also includes animal husbandry and fishery that can be dovetailed to forestry and agriculture, paying adequate attention to ecological aspects and the dynamics of energy flow. For this study, 1 acre plot of usar land in village Trilokpur was chosen for developing agroforestry specially for fuelwood and fodder plantations.

The following steps were taken :

(1) Dividing the selected patch of land into different sized plots.

(2) Preparing bunds by pada bunding.

(3) Making provision for collecting rain water during the monsoon period.

(4) Leaching out the salts from the soil during the first year.

(5) Applying farmyard manure, avoiding chemical fertilizers.

(6) Arranging irrigation facility through tubewell for ensuring continuous supply of green fodder.

(7) Planting subabool (*Leucaena leucocephala*), Hawaian Giant variety, first in polypot, raised pits or saucer pan, so that salts get leached out through gravity flow.

(8) Planting trees at 1.6×1.6 m spacing for fuelwood production.

(9) Interplanting trees at 4×1 m spacing with cultivated fodder crop after usar land has been partially reclaimed.

(10) Interplanting subabool, a leguminous tree, with lucerne (Rizka), a cultivated leguminous fodder crop, which increases the overall nutrient content in the soil in terms of nitrogen level markedly.

(11) Seeds from harvested crops being salt tolerant should be used subsequently in the same reclaimed land.

(12) Using reclaimed land for growing wheat-cum-fennel seed and other crops.

(13) Taking up land for cultivation of foodgrain crops and cash crops after a period of 3-5 years, depending on the fertility status of the soil.

(14) Irrigating the cultivated crops on rotation, which also helps to irrigate trees.

(15) Making provision for protective irrigation of trees.

4.4 Reclaiming Wastelands for Forestry

Attempts to grow trees in highly sodic soils have been largely unsuccessful. Some scientists have presented results of field experiments to show that species such as Eucalyptus, Prosopis and *Acacia nilotica* could be grown in highly alkali soils, if the soil in 90×90 m pit was improved through application of gypsum and farmyard manure. Recent studies have shown that if tree seedlings are planted in auger holes filled with a mixture of original soil, 3-4 kg gypsum and 7-8 kg farmyard manure, excellent growth is achieved. In the present study, a favourable environment for root growth was created in a limited area to a depth of 180 cm in village Teri of Amethi Block. The main objective of this study was to examine the feasibility of using afforestation technology in usar land. The following are among the measures needed for the reclamation of usar land with high soil pH for afforestation programmes :

(1) Measuring the pH of the soil to know the nature of the soil and strata of the *kankar* pan.

(2) Arranging irrigation facility before taking up afforestation work.

(3) Breaking and removing *kankar* pan of the pit.

(4) Digging pits at 1×1×1 m or 60×60×60 cm spacing.

(5) Taking out soil of the pit up to 0.5 m depth and replacing it with soil of appropriate pH adding to it farmyard manure and pyrite in appropriate proportions.

(6) Leaching out along with rain water salts responsible for the salinity of the soil.

(7) Applying farmyard manure, pyrite/gypsum, nitrogen and zinc sulphate to reduce the salinity of the soil.

(8) Planting Prosopis in a selected patch of usar land.

(9) Doing pad bunding of small plots.

(10) Providing live hedge aud trench fencing.

(11) Providing adequate irrigation facilities in the form of tubewell to ensure availability of sweet water.

(12) Weeding and fertilization at appropriate times.

(13) Digging suitable drainage lines for the removal of excess water and flushing out the salinity of the soil.

4.5 Conclusion

It follows from the above discussion that by suitably modifying wasteland reclamation measures, the requirements of any type of soil can be met so as to make it suitable for agriculture, agroforestry or forestry. While working out a reclamation plan, adequate attention should be paid to levelling of the land, drainage improvement and ample supply of irrigation water of good quality. Projects on wasteland reclamation, big or small, can be economic propositions if they are planned on scientific lines. Shooting up of land prices and scarcity of cultivable land have lent urgency to reclamation programmes. While the general reclamation procedure is very simple, appropriate management practices have to be developed for specific situations, with particular attention to proper selection of crops, planting and irrigation techniques. It is also essential to take proper decisions regarding the purpose for which the wastcland is to be reclaimed—agriculture, agroforestry or forestry.

The following sub-practices need to be optimized :

(a) Land preparation and tillage.

(b) Seed bed preparation and planting.

(c) Irrigation, leaching and drainage.

(d) Crop rotation.

(e) Continuous cropping.

(f) Application of amendments.

(g) Afforestation and pasture development.

(h) Collection of seeds of the harvested crop and their subsequent use in the same land.

(i) Application of adequate quantities of fertilizers, manure and zinc sulphate.

(j) Adoption of appropriate cultural and agronomic practices.

(k) Use of good quality water and proper water management practices.

Apart from the above-mentioned reclamation methods, certain preventive measures and management practices should also be adopted. There are also some other important measures, such as intensive pre-irrigation, soil surveys and mapping of sub-soil characteristics, in respect of permeability and identification of the areas, where water table is expecled to rise. By adopting these measures, it is possible to extend the net cultivated area.

It may be concluded that large-scale chemical treatment of wastelands for their reclamation is not necessary. Simple bunding and levelling coupled with nutrient replenishment by planting leguminous trees, specially for fuelwood and fodder, gives excellent results. The returns are sufficiently higher with agroforestry than with forestry and agriculture, because agroforestry provides cultivated fodder, fuelwood and grains. Fuelwood plantations interplanted with cultivated fodder plants generate substantial income from the second year onwards. Wastelands with low pH of the soil may be reclaimed for agricultural use, those with medium pH for agroforestry and finally those with high pH value for forestry according to the fertility status of the soil. Through judicious decisions, the productivity can be increased substantially. The returns from investments made on the reclamation of wastelands are sufficiently high. Besides increasing the net sown area, it helps in increasing the supply of foodgrains, fuelwood and fodder for the rural poor. Wasteland reclamation projects have the potential to provide benefits not only to the human population but to the cattle population as well. They generate employment for the landless rural poor and help in improving their socio-economic status.

5

Economic Viability of Wastelands Reclamation

5.1 Introduction

Any attempt to reclaim wastelands can be taken to be essential and worth while from the point of view of economic development through increase in agricultural production by bringing additional area under cultivation. While the pressure of human and cattle population is increasing rapidly, extension of cultivated land has been stagnant for several years. The main reason for this is that exploitation of such uncultivated lands has not been within the reach of the ordinary farmer. Most of these lands are not suitable for agricultural use. Reclamation of any type of wasteland is a time-consuming and costly affair. Adoption of such measures for wastelands as accentuate soil erosion is not desirable from the long-term point of view. In view of the above constraints, it is essential that the pros and cons of wasteland reclamation are made amply clear to the farmers, so that they adopt the most appropriate remedial measures. Though high expenditure is involved in practising most of the remedial measures in the initial stages, subsequently the farmers begin to derive considerable benefit from the reclaimed lands. The farmers can be induced to go in for reclamation of wastelands only by disseminating to them information regarding the economic benefits in the form of additional agricultural production, which ultimately paves the way for socio-economic development of the region.

The economics of reclamation of various wasteland types is closely linked to the management aspect. The cost of reclamation depends upon the nature and extent of degradation the concerned wasteland has undergone. Here, an attempt has been made to work out the average expenditure involved in the reclamation of 1 acre (0.4 hectare) wastelands of different types. Three types of wastelands (usar land) were selected for reclamation according to their suitability for agriculture, agroforestry or forestry after reclamation. The broad criterion in this respect was to reclaim usar lands with soil of high pH for forestry, those of medium pH for agroforestry and those of low pH for agriculture. The input-output analysis was done after reclamation of each wasteland type.

The main factors that need to be taken into consideration in attempting to reclaim a wasteland are the cost of reclamation and the anticipated benefits in terms of additional foodgrains, fodder and fuelwood produced. The economics of reclamation of different wasteland types was worked out with the cooperation of farmers and concerned government officials of the block and the district.

5.2 Economics of Wasteland Reclamation for Agriculture

The main operations involved in the reclamation of usar land with soil of low pH are levelling, bunding, land preparation, leaching, flushing, and application of gypsum/pyrite. The type and quantity of fertilizer to be used depends on the requirement of the soil. Hence, the cost of reclamation also varies with the extent of usarization and the prevailing cost of commodities and labour.

Usar land with reh encrustation has a high content of soluble salts. White encrustations and powder appear on the soil surface in the summer season. Such usar land can be reclaimed by leaching and flushing with good quality water, ensuring proper drainage. The expected benefits and the encouragement provided by government have induced the cultivators to reclaim and manage their private owned usar land for crop production. Therefore, it is important to make a concurrent assessment of reclamation technology for usar land in terms of input requirement, possible output and benefits. This would help in formulating suitable reclamation policies in relation to credit requirement, returns and repayment capacity. Based on past experience at cultivators' fields, the cost-benefit analysis has been done during both Kharif and Rabi seasons.

Usar land reclamation work was done in village Danapur. The work involved leaching and flushing with good quality water. Adequate attention was paid to improvement of the drainage system.

As per the data given in Table 5.1, the cost of reclaiming and sowing paddy crop in 1 acre of usar land with predominantly high sodium content and soil pH above 8.5 works out to Rs 2175. Such usar lands are characterized by block encrustations appearing on dry soil surface. The abovementioned expenditure on reclaiming usar land in the first Kharif season includes that on levelling and bunding, land preparation, gypsum application, impounding of water, fertilizer, plant protection, irrigation, harvesting and threshing. It is seen from Table 5.2 that the value of paddy produced in the first Kharif season works out to Rs 2940 (Rs 2610 from the grain and Rs 330 from the straw). Thus, against an investment of Rs 2175 in the first Kharif season, the profit from reclamation of 1 acre usar land comes to Rs 765.

In the second season of reclamation cycle in the same field, wheat crop was sown. The total expenditure incurred on reclamation, which involved land preparation, costs of seedings, fertilizers, irrigation, harvesting and threshing works out to Rs 1550 (Table 5.3). It is seem from Table 5.4 that the return has been Rs 3610 (Rs 2800 from grain and Rs 810 from straw), giving a clear profit of Rs 2026.

Thsse are very encouraging results. In fact, the returns can be expected to be still higher in the successive season.

5.3 Economics of Wasteland Reclamation for Agroforestry

For working out the economics of wasteland reclamation

Table 5.1—Capital Requirement for Reclamation of Usar Land (1 Acre)

(The deta are for paddy crop in Kharirf season)

Sl No.	Operation	Human labour man-days	Wages paid Rs	Expenditure on draught power employed* Rs	Cost of inputs: Material/ operation	Cost of inputs: Quantity	Cost of inputs: Amount paid Rs	Total expen- diture Rs
1	Levelling and bunding	8	112	30				142
2	Land preparation	5	70	90				160
3	Gypsum application	5	70		Gypsum	40	300	370
4	Impounding of water	2	28		Irrigation	—	80	80
5	Fertilizer application	3	42		Urea	60 kg	180	
					Shakti khad	30 kg	90	462
					M. Potash	40 kg	70	
					Compost	—	80	
6	Transplanting of seed-lings, including nursery cost	15	210		Paddy seedling	—	350	460
7	Cultural practices	1	14		—		—	14

8	Top dressing of fertilizer	1	14	Urea	25 kg	75	89
9	Plant protection	1	14	$ZnSO_4$ and Blito	—	60	60
10	Irrigation	2	28	Tubewell	6 h	72	72
11	Harvesting	10	140				140
12	Threshing	9					126
	Total expenditure						2175

* Hire charges for a pair of bullocks and plough @ Rs 3/h.

5.2—Output per Acre in Kharif Season from Reclaimed Usar Land

Crop	Yield		Prevailing price		Value of output		Total output Rs	Profit Rs
	Grain	Straw	Grain	Straw	Grain	Straw		
Paddy	18	15	145	22	2610	330	2940	1125

Table 5.3—Capital Requirement during the Second Reclamation Cycle

(The data are for wheat crop in Rabi Season)

Sl No.	Operation	Human labour man-days	Wages paid Rs	Draught employed payment Rs	Cost of inputs: Material/ operation	Qty	Cost Rs	Total expenditure on draught power* Rs
1	Land preparation	8	112	120	—		—	232
2	Seedling	4	56	40	Wheat		320	426
3	Fertilizer application				Urea	60 kg	180	
					M. potash	50 kg	150	400
					Phosphate	40 kg	70	
4	Cultural practices	3	42		—		—	42
5	Top dressing of fertilizer	2	28		Urea	3 kg	90	118
6	Irrigation	6	84		Tubewell	35 h	280	364
7	Harvesting	12	168		irrigation			168
8	Threshing	8	112		Machine	6 h	72	184
	Total expenditure							1550

* Hire charges for a pair of bullocks and plough @ Rs 3/h.

Table 5.4—Output per Acre in Rabi Season from the Reclaimed Land

Crop	Yield		Prevailing prices		Value of output		Total output	Profit
	Grain	Straw	Grain	Straw	Grain	Straw	Rs	Rs
	q	q	Rs/q	Rs/q	Rs	Rs		
Wheat	16	18	175	45	2880	810	3610	2060

for agroforestry, village Trilokpur of Amethi Block was chosen. The selected patch of wasteland has been classified as usar land in village records. Reclamation of usar land for agroforestry involves the following major steps :

(i) Proper levelling and bunding for harvesting rain water and pounding the land with rain water.

(ii) Planting subabool at 4×1 m spacing along with cultivated fodder (mixed plantation).

(iii) Creation of proper irrigation sources by constructing tubewells to ensure continuous supply of water needed to grow green fodder throughout the year.

In the present study, the fixed capital expenditure on creation of irrigation facility (tubewells) was avoided. Rather, water supply was arranged from private sources against payment.

Details of expenditure incurred during the first year on site preparation, purchase of plants, seeds, replanting, weeding, purchase of fertilizer and its application, irrigation, purchase of implements, etc. are given in Table 5.5. Being a

Table 5.5—Estimated Expenditure on Raising Agroforestry Plantation on Wastelands

(Data are for 1 acres plantation in usar land)

Sl No.	Operation	Particulars	Expenditure Rs
1	Site preparation	25 man-days	350
2	Alignment and stacking	15 days	210
3	Cost of plants along with fodder	30 paisa per plant	900
4	Mixed planting and replanting	20 paisa per plant	1500
5	Weeding	2 q; 12 man-days	168
6	Application of fertilizer	FYM	90
7	Fire protection	2 man-days	15
8	Hand tools	—	40
9	Irrigation cost	—	200
10	Contingencies	—	115
	Total		3588

pilot study, investment on sophisticated equipment was avoided. The poor farmers too cannot afford these.

After one year, the trees are coppiced. Expenditures incurred on weeding, fertilization, fire protection and irrigation are recurring items. After coppicing in the third year, the tree attains the same growth in the 5th year: coppiced then, it once again is ready for reharvesting in the 8th year. The total cycle up to which a subabool tree can be coppiced is considered to be of 15 years' duration. Mixed plantation of subabool and cultivated fodder involved an expenditure of Rs 3588 for 1 acre usar land during the first year. Different varieties of nutritious green and dry fodder as well as grain-cum-fodder crop were cultivated. A sum of Rs 240 was expended on growing fodder crop in reclaimed 1 acre of usar land during both Kharif and Rabi seasons.

Income from subabool has been envisaged in the form of leaves, timber and seeds. This income has been assumed and is expected to be achieved in the forthcoming years. Input-output analysis has been done based on earlier experiences on successful reclamation and growing of trees and fodder crops. Statistics on expected income from agroforestry plantation are given in Table 5.6. The income from 1 acre reclaimed

Table 5.6—Expected Income from Agroforestry Plantation on Wastelands

Sl No.	Item	Income Rs
1	Trees	
	(a) Leaves	360
	(b) Timber	4600
	(c) Seed	800
2	Fodder	
	(a) Green	800
	(b) Dry	450
3	Seeds	350
	Profit	2972

usar land in the first year is Rs 6500 (Rs 360 from leaves, Rs 4600 from timber, Rs 800 from seeds from the trees, Rs 1250 from green and dry fodder and Rs 350 from fodder seed). On coppicing, a tree is expected to yield 9 kg of biomass on dry weight basis every three years. Thus, the total return expected from 1 acre reclaimed usar land for developing agroforestry plantation is Rs 2972 against an expenditure of Rs 3588. The agroforestry plantation starts generating surplus from third year onwards.

5.4 Economics of Wasteland Reclamation for Forestry

Reclamation of usar land requires considerable capital investment in the first year of reclamation. This one-time expenditure includes that on installation of tubewell, land levelling, bunding of land, flooding and application of gypsum as amendment. The item-wise breakup of capital requirement for usar land reclamation for afforestation is given in Table 5.7. The total investment on reclamation of 1

Table 5.7—Capital Requirement for Forestry Development

Sl No.	Operation	Expenditure Rs
1	Survey and site preparation	28
2	Trenching, levelling and bunding	175
3	Digging of pits for plantation (60 man-days)	840
4	Filling of the pits with sand, good quality soil, organic and inorganic manures	325
5	Nursery cost	550
6	Carriage of plants	15
7	Plantation	180
8	Maintenance of roads and paths	56
9	Irrigation	200
10	Supply of material and equipment	120
11	Miscellaneous and unforeseen expenses	150
	Total	2519

acre usar land for forestry during the first year works out to Rs 2519. In subsequent years, nominal expenditure has to be incurred on maintenance of plants. In a few cases, replanting may be necessary, but this needs very little expenditure. The plantations start giving returns after 5-6 years. Based on the previous experience gained from tree plantation, it is assumed that a 1 acre plantation will start giving an annual return of Rs 6500 from the sixth year onwards. The direct benefits of afforestation would come through both major and minor products. In this exercise, wood for fuel purposes is considered to be the direct benefit. The final output in terms of fuelwood is assumed to be 30 tonnes per acre. These estimates are based on an yield of 35 kg air-dried fuelwood per ***Eucalyptus tereticornis*** tree.

5.5 Conclusion

The present study has established the financial and economic viability of crop production, agroforestry and forestry in usar land. However, the profitability of these ventures depends upon proper management. Choice of the most appropriate crops/trees is an essential step. The main factors influencing the economics of reclamation are the inputs needed to reclaim the wastelands and the anticipated benefits in terms of production. Initial cost of wasteland reclamation is high, but with proper phasing based on good management practices, returns are fairly high after two years. By inter-planting fuelwood plantation with cultivated fodder, high returns can be obtained. High doses of chemical amendment are not very necessary for moderate usar lands. Measures like simple levelling, bunding, trenching, leaching and flushing, coupled with nutrient replenishment through planting of leguminous trees and cultivated fodder and addition of farmyard manure, give excellent results. Maximum returns are achieved from mixed plantation.

6

Strategies for Reclamation of Wastelands

6.1 Introduction

Having discussed the distribution of wastelands of Amethi Block, their distinctive features and the costs involved in their reclamation for different purposes—agriculture, agroforestry or forestry—an attempt has been made in this chapter to suggest strategies to be adopted for obtaining the best results under different situations. For any venture of this type, it is necessary to devote adequate attention to policy formulation and then its implementation. The importance of managerial resources too cannot be underestimated. Management implies the way responsibility is delegated and decisions made, the way functions are differentiated and coordinated, the way managers are selected, promoted and rewarded and the way information is disseminated to the right persons at the right time. And the most important thing is to ensure proper integration of various activities to achieve the best possible results. Thus, the strategy related to management and structure building for wasteland utiljzation plays an important role in the overall development of rural areas, especially through the reclamation of wastelands. The importance of management is not in knowing but in doing. Its test is not logic but in results.

In practical terms, the strategies to be adopted include provision of packets of the most suitable technological inputs, credit support, building up of a strong social infrastructure and arranging marketing support. In planning for the development of wastelands, due attention also needs to be paid to the supporting activities like motivation of poor farmers and persons of weaker sections, including landless farmers, to adopt appropriate technology and organization of the distribution system for meeting the minimum needs of the weaker sections in respect of such inputs as they cannot manage on their own.

It has to be noted that so far no organised effort has been made by any central or block level government agency to formulate action oriented planning strategies for effective utilization of wasteland resources. As a result of this, such lands continue to be put to sub-optimal use and in many cases to even destructive use. Thus, while on one hand the rural poor are to be motivated to participate in these programmes, on the other an active role of the concerned governmental agencies has to be ensured. By restoring the productivity of wastelands, the socio-economic status of the people will go up and at the same time the ecological balance will be maintained.

6.2 Major Components of Wasteland Reclamation Programmes

(I) Identification of the problem

The first essential task is identification of the wastelands problem at micro-and meso-levels. For this, it is necessary to undertake a district-wise, village-wise or even plot-wise wastelands and soil survey and to draw maps indicating their detailed distribution. It is equally important to gather information on proportionate distribution and growth of various wasteland types at village level through the involvement of village accountants, village heads, interested farmers, personnel of the Soil Conservation Department, Revenue Department, District Agricultural Officers and Block Development Officers.

(2) Determinants of Wastelands

The next important step is to identify the factors responsible for the formation of wastelands.

(3) Genesis of the Wastelands

On the basis of the identified determinants of wastelands, the genesis of the problem should be studied in the context of the status of the wasteland in question, i.e., the extent of degradation it has undergone. This means classification of lands into three categories : marginally, partially and severely deteriorated lands. The strategy to be worked out will depend on the category to which a particular wasteland belongs.

(4) Capability Classification

The next major step is categorization of wastelands on the basis of their capability for reclamation. This will then form the basis for evolving models for action plans. The capability classification should be based on factors like determinants of wastelands, genesis of the problem, limitations of resources, location of the affected areas, etc.

(5) Action-oriented Planning

Within a specified timeframe, the concerned government agencies should prepare and make available a reliable database for various wasteland types after their identification and suitability for different purposes—agriculture, agroforestry or forestry.

Government officials and voluntary agencies are required to assist the farmers, particularly in the demonstration of improved methods of cultivation and in arranging supply of the requisite inputs for the reclamation of wasteland for various purposes. This includes arranging for loans for the small, marginal and landless farmers and people from the weaker sections of the society to enable them to acquire the needed implements. Another essential component of the programme is an organized publicity campaign, integrated with programmes for training the farmers and government officials at various levels on various aspects of wasteland utilization. The scientists can play an effective role by suggesting necessary changes in cropping patterns, particularly for drought prone and desert areas, where there are serious moisture stress-related bottlenecks in the work of programmes concerned with wasteland reclamation. Other tasks for the scientists include selection of appropriate species of crops, fodder and trees according to the nature of the wasteland in question, making provision for adequate supply of seeds of high yielding varieties, requisite extension support pertaining to choice of cropping pattern, methods of cropping, harvesting and marketing.

Various government agencies concerned with integrated rural development programmes should ensure supply of raw materials, on subsidized basis, wherever justified. This is particularly necessary in respect of gypsum/pyrite and other organic or inorganic amendments needed for the reclamation of wastelands of different types.

The soil testing laboratories, including the mobile ones, should ensure prompt and accurate testing of soils. In addition, they should provide guidance to the farmers on the use of organic and inorganic amendments according to the nature and requirement of the soil.

Hydrologic scientists from various agencies should visit the villages to advise the farmers in respect of simple but better water management steps for checking soil erosion and overflow of water, which damage the fertility status of the soil.

Proper facilities needed for augmenting irrigation facilities should be made available to the farmers in respect of programmes related to reclamation of wastelands. They should also be provided guidance regarding control of waterlogging and the consequential usarization.

Cooperative societies of farmers, voluntary organizations, and enlightened individual farmers should be provided all needed encouragement and incentives in relation to wasteland development programmes.

Appropriate technologies for wasteland reclamation should be made available to persons belonging to weaker sections and landless farmers.

Mining activity should be curbed in such areas where it is leading to growth of wastelands. Steps should be taken to find alternative sources of such essential raw materials whose supply gets interrupted due to this. Collective efforts need to be made to check soil losses through water and wind erosion and to prevent the collapse of irrigation system through siltation.

Plans concerning wasteland reclamation and utilization prepared at various levels should be properly integrated. Action in respect of various operations related to reclamation should be coordinated keeping in view the capapility and suitability of the wasteland for various purposes—agriculture, agroforestry and forestry.

6.3 Strategies for Wasteland Development

Optimum strategies, structures and policies should be devised and adopted, so that wastelands are reclaimed through integrated use of various skills related to increase in food, fuelwood and fodder production through greening of the wastelands.

Coordinating agencies should be established, if necessary even at village level, to help the poor farmers is having access to the needed technological inputs and preventing the formation of wastelands. Another function of these agencies would be to create awareness among farmers about various reclamation measures.

District level officials should help the farmers is acquiring wastelands on lease, equipment and various technological inputs, market information and information related matters as well as in the marketing of their produce.

Imaginative strategies for communication with farmers should be organized and extended. Appropriate use of various mass media, such as radio and television, local newspapers, films and various audiovisual techniques should be made to motivate the farmers to participate enthusiastically in programmes relating to reclamation and greening of wastelands. Just like the green revolution, there should be a programme for "Greening of Wasteland" with active involvement of R & D organizations, extension agencies, voluntary organizations and the farmers.

People's involvement is necessary in all operations like nursery farming, forestry, tree patta system, land patta system, etc. Provision should be there for giving proper incentives to the farmers.

6.4 Structures for Wasteland Development

The selected patch of wasteland should be properly levelled to ensure uniform application of irrigation water, fertilizers and organic and inorganic amendments. Further, the land should be divided into plots of appropriate sizes to ensure adequate levelling and proper bunding.

The bunds made should be strong enough to check the entry of run-off water from outside as well as to prevent outflow of the water from the field. Surface drainge should be provided outside the bund to ensure proper outfow of the water during the reclaiming operation. Use should be made of rain water during rainy season to leach out undesirable compounds from the soil. Good quality water should be used for irrigational purposes.

Soil should be tested for its proper characterization and determining the requirement of organic and inorganic amendments for increasing the productivity. Gypsum and pyrite are ideal amendments; these are to be added in the upper 10 cm layer with light ploughing, 15-20 days before paddy crop.

After amendment of soil, irrigation should be done freely, so that up to 5-7 cm water level is obtained. Green manuring before and after cultivation helps to maintain the fertility status of the soil.

Depending upon the soil type and the environmental conditions, wastelands can be developed for forestry, agroforestry or agriculture. In many cases, no extensive physical and chemical reclamation techniques except bunding the area and pounding with rain water are required.

If the land is not suitable for growing agricultural crops, growing of leguminous tree species is recommended for improving the fertility status of the soil. Subabool, a leguminous tree, besides being salt-tolerant, helps in fixation of nitrogen. Once forestry or agroforestry is developed, the land can be taken up for cultivation of grain crops or cash crops after a period of 3-7 years, depending on the extent of usarization of the land in the beginning.

Irrigation facilities are to be provided only for cultivated crops. There is no need for separate irrigation facilities for tree plantations ; protective irrigation is sufficient for them. Irrigation sources like tubewells are to be created in selected patches of wastelands for reclamation. Trees for fuelwood should be planted at 1.5×1.5 m spacing. In the case of mixed plantations, trees should be planted at 4×1 m spacing along with cultivated fodder. Seeds of the crops harvested should be collected and used for growing subsequent crop in the same land, because plants growing from such seeds are more salt-tolerant and productivity of the crop in that case is higher in comparison to that of crop obtained by sowing seeds secured from outside.

The reclaimed land can be used for growing wheat, cumin and fennel plants and various fodder crops.

In terms of financial returns, mixed cultivation (fuelwood trees and cultivated fodder) is more profitable than agricultural production.

6.5 Extension Programme

Due attention should be paid to the organization of training, demonstration and extension programmes for creating awareness among weaker sections in remote interior villages on various aspects of wasteland reclamation programmes.

7

Conclusions

The growing demand of the increasing human population for goods and services has imposed severe pressures on the available natural resources, especially on the forest and green cover. This situation is also closely linked to the quality of life of the rural masses who constitute 75% of the nation's population. The increasing demand for food, fibre, fruits, fodder, fuelwood, fishery products and other materials to meet the growing needs of the population and industries has led to activities responsible for increasing environmental degradation and rapid extension of wastelands. Presently, India has as high as 1.75 million ha degraded land out of the total land area of 328 million ha. Satellite imagery indicates that we are losing about 1.3 million ha of forest every year. The Prime Minister has given the call to bring 5 million ha of land every year under fuelwood and fodder plantations and to generate a people's movement for afforestation. Thus, development of agriculture, agroforestry and forestry has become an essential prerequisite for the overall socio-economic development of the country. It is imperative to extend the area under cultivation to the maximum possible extent for increasing the production of food, fuelwood and fodder.

In the Indian context, pressure on land is already very high and the only hope for extending the net sown area as well as increasing forest area lies in bringing improvement in various categories of wastelands, particularly fallow lands other than fallow and culturable wastelands. The preliminary steps to be taken in this direction are :

(1) Systematic study of the physical characteristics of wastelands of different categories and assessment of the possibilities of their management, and

(2) cost-benefit analysis of reclamation of these lands.

With the above considerations in view, the following objectives were set for the present study conducted in respect of the wastelands of Amethi Block of Sultanpur District in UP.

(1) to study the distribution of wastelands at village level,

(2) to study the trends of growth of wastelands in Sultanpur District and Amethi Block during the periods 1977-78 to 1981-82 and 1981-82 to 1986-87.

(3) to identify the environmental and anthropogenic factors responsible for the formation of various types of wastelands,

(4) to study various correlates of wastelands at village level.

(5) to work out suitable strategies for the reclamation of wastelands, especially for forestry, agroforestry and agriculture,

(6) to work out the economics of wasteland reclamation, and

(7) to suggest suitable action plans for effective utilization of wastelands.

The wastelands of Amethi Block fall into six types– waterlogged, usar, banjar, old fallow, and other types of wastelands.

The proportion of wastelands in Sultanpur District is quite high (12.8% of the total area of the district in 1977-78). During 1977-78 to 1981-82, it increased by 10.93%, making the area of wastelands 13.2% of the total area. By 1986-87, through a further increase of 3.35%, it had reached 14.18% of the total area. The proportion of wastelands in Amethi Block was 8.64% of the total area in 1977-78; it had increased to 9.23% by 1981-82 and to 9.71% by 1986-87. Thus, the rate of growth has been 9.92% during 1977-78 to 1981-82 and 4.18% during 1981-82 to 1986-87. These statistics indicate a positive change, but a slowing in this change is perceptible. The main reason for this positive change is that some of the wastelands have begun to be utilized for various purposes. On the whole, however, the area of wastelands has been increasing.

All the villages of the block have wastelands; their extent, however, varies from village to village. About 55% of the villages have less than 12% of their area under wastelands.

An attempt has been made to make a quantitative study of the impact of different determinants which have been generally responsible for the variation in the proportion of different types of wastelands in the block. A summary of the results of stepwise regression analysis given in Table 7.1 brings out the relative roles of different variables in relation to the variation in area under different categories of wastelands as percentage of the total area.

A thorough investigation has been made of the possible measures for reclaiming wastelands of different types for various purposes. For this, three types of usar land were chosen for their reclamation for forestry, agroforestry and agriculture.

Table 7.1—Determinants of Distribution of Wasteland of Different Types

Sl. No.	Type of wasteland	Important variable	Other contributory variables
1	Waterlogged	Slope	Drainage density
2	Usar	pH of soil	Land concentration
3	Banjar	do	—
4	Old fallow	do	—
5	Fallow	Quality of water (pH)	Drainage density
6	Other types of wastelands	Land concentration	—
7	Total wasteland	pH of soil	Land concentration, drainage density, behaviour of water table

In each of three selected villages, 1 acre of affected land was taken up for reclamation to find out the efficacy of different reclamation measures. The study was conducted over a period of one year. The basic steps in the reclamation procedure were :

(1) Proper land levelling, bunding, leaching and flushing.

(2) Application of suitable chemical amendments in right quantities and in a proper manner as per requirements of the concerned land.

(3) Choice of salt-tolerant crops in a proper sequence and in variety.

(4) Adoption of appropriate cultural and agronomic practices.

(5) Proper water management and use of good quality water.

Reclamation of usar lands with soils of low pH was aimed at making them fit for agriculture. In the first Kharif season, paddy crop was sown followed by wheat in the second season. Usar lands with soils of intermediate pH were intended to be used for agroforestry after reclamation. In these lands, subabool plantations were raised, putting plants at 1.6×1.6 m spacing, when the main objective was production of fuelwood. In mixed plantations, subabool was inter-planted with lucerne (Rizka), a cultivated leguminous fodder crop. Usar lands with soils of high pH were earmarked for afforestation purpose. In these lands, eucalyptus, prosopis, acacia and subabool trees were planted at $1 \times 1 \times 1$ m spacing. The economics of reclamation was worked out only in the case of eucalyptus plantation.

Based on the results of the present study, suggestions have been made in respect of appropriate cultural, agronomic and water management practices relating to different situations. Of course, the reclamation measures suggested have to be suitably modified to meet the specific requirements of a particular soil.

The general conclusion from the present study is that reclamation of any type of wasteland can be an economic proposition, if the project is carried out on scientific lines. In so far as the economics of reclamation of usar land is concerned, the calculations made in the present study indicate that by growing paddy crop in the first Kharif season, a total earning of Rs 2940 per acre can be expected, giving a net profit of Rs 1125. In the following Rabi season, from wheat crop, a profit of Rs 2060 per acre can be expected.

Agroforestry plantation in 1 acre usar land can provide an estimated income, aiter a few years, of Rs 2972 per year, including that from trees, leaves, timber, green and dry fodder and seeds useble for replanting. On the whole, agroforestry plantation programme appears to be economically more beneficial than the other reclamation programmes.

The cost of reclamation varies from one type of wasteland to another. The benefit depends on the inputs, type of crop sown and management of various reclamation measures. In general, the returns increase as the cycle of reclamation progresses.

Suggestions and Strategies

(1) For locating wastelands and identifying the factors responsible for their growth, pilot projects should be taken up in areas where wastelands are widely distributed. Depending upon the nature and capability of a particular patch of wasteland, specific reclamation strategies and plans should be worked out, keeping in view the use to which the reclaimed land is to be put, viz. agroforestry, forestry or agriculture.

(2) Action-oriented planning for the reclamation of wastelands should be done with the involvement of farmers and local government and non-government officials.

(3) Due attention should be paid to such aspects as augmentation of irrigation facilities, timely and adequate supply of various needed inputs, particularly in the case of poor and landless farmers.

(4) Committees soould be constituted at village level to undertake wasteland developmental planning for various purposes with the involvement of village, block and district level officials.

(5) Pragmatic strategies should be evolved and implemented for motivating the farmers to take up wasteland development work in a big way. 'Greening of wastelands' should be transformed inro a people's programme. This calls for wide publicity at different levels.

(6) Adequate arrangements should be made to organize demonstrations of reclamation measures in each village.

(7) All needed technological inputs should be made available to the poor farmers.

(8) The economics of wasteland reclamation must be explained to the poor farmers in a manner which has the potential to enthuse them to take up wasteland reclamation work with vigour.

(9) Once fhe reclamation projects are initiated, the responsibility for the followup actions should be discharged by the staff of the concerned departments (agriculture, soil conservation, etc.) with full sincerity and dedication.

Bibliography

(1) BOOKS

Anderson, JR, *A geography of agriculture* (Durbuque, Iowa), 1971.

Bali JS, *Ravine reclamation needs for India* (New Delhi), 1972.

Bennett HH, *Elements of soil conservation*, (McGraw Hill Book Co., New York), 1955.

Bhattacharya JP, *Study of soil conservation for agricultural land* (New Delhi), 1964.

Blandford HF, *The climates and weather of India, Ceylon and Burma* (London), 1889.

Browrigg FW, *Settlement report, District Sultanpur*. 1898.

Chaudhari, P (ed), *Readings in Indian agricultural development* (George Allen and Unwin Ltd., London), 1972.

Chauhan DS, *Studies in utilisation of agricultural land* (Aggarawala Publishers, Agra), 1966.

Chislom M, *Rural settlement and land use* (Hutchinson Lib), 1962.

Ganguli HN, *Restoration of soil structures with gypsum* (Bikaner Gypsum Ltd, Bikaner). 1954.

Govinda Rajan SV & Gopala Rao HG. *Studies on soils of India* (New Delhi), 1978.

Gregor, HF, *Agricultural geography, themes in research* (Prentice Hall Ltd, London), 1970.

Hadimani, AS, *Studies on the wastelands of Delhi state*, M. Sc. Associate, Indian Agricultural Research Institute, New Delhi, 1960.

Hall A, *The soil*, (London), 1947.

Hartshorne A, *Perspective on the nature of geography* (Dutler and Tanner, London), 1959.

Johnston J, *Economic methods* (MacGraw Hill Book Co., New York), 1972.

Kelley WP, *The climates of continents* (Oxford University Press, Oxford), 1927.

Kendall MG, *A course in multi-variate analysis* (Charles Griffin, London), 1957.

King Thomson, *Water miracles of nature* (MacMillans & Co., New York), 1953.

Kostrowickly J, *Hierarchy of world types of agriculture* (Poland), 1979.

Kostrowicki J, *Land utilisation in East Central Europe Case studies* (Geographia Polnica, 5, Warsaw, Poland). 1965.

Krishnan MS, *Geology of India and Burma* (Madras). 1960.

Leather JW, *Investigation of usar lands in the United Provinces* (Government Press, Allahabad), 1914.

Mahmood Aslam, *Statistical methods in geographical studies* (Rajesh Publications, New Delhi), 1977.

Medicott HB & Blanford HF, *Manual of geology of India* 1879.

Mitra, Ashok & Mukherjee, Sheikher, Population, food and land inequality in India, in *A geography of hunger and insecurity, an ICSSAR/JNU/FPF Study*, (Allied Publishers Pvt. Ltd., New Delhi), 1980.

Mohammad Ali, *Studies in agricultural geography* (Rajesh Publishers, New Delhi), 1978.

Mohammad Ali, *Dynamics of agricultural development in India* (Concept Publishing Co., New Delhi), 1978.

Monk House, FJ & Wilkinson HR, *Maps and diagram*, 2nd edn (University Paperbacks, Methuen and Co. Ltd., London), 1964.

Mooreland HH, *The agriculture of United Provinces* (Allahabad), 1912.

Moore WG, *A dictionary of geography* (Penguin Books, London), 1976.

Munshull R, *Regional geography* (Hutchinson Lib., London), 1967.

Nevill HR, *District Gazetteer of the District Sultanpur* (Allahabad), 1903.

Nigam NM, *How to reclaim saline and alkali lands in the Delhi state*, Thesis Associate, Indian Agricultural Research Institute, New Delhi, 1956.

Pilai VR & Panikar PGK, *Land reclamation in Kerala* (Asia Publishing House, New Delhi), 1965.

Porter FW, *Final settlement report of the Sultanpur District, North Western Provinces and Oudh* (Allahabad), 1888.

Raheja PC, *Soil productivity and crop growth* (Asia Publishing House, New Delhi), 1966.

Rao KL, *India's water wealth : Its assessmet, uses and projections* (Orient Longman, New Delhi), 1979.

Raychaudhuri SP, *Soils of India* (New Delhi) 1962.

Raychaudhuri SP, *Land and soil* (National Book Trust, New Delhi), 1966.

Robinson GM, *Mother earth* (London), 1937.

Shafi M, *Land utilisation in Eastern Uttar Pradesh* (Aligarh Muslim University, Aligarh), 1960.

Sharma HS, *Ravine erosion in India* (Concept Publishing Co, New Delhi), 1980.

Sharma PS. *Agricultural regionalisation of India* (New Heights Publishers and Distributors, Delhi), 1973.

Shome KB & Raychudhury SP, *Rating of soils of India* (Indian Agricultural Research Institute, New Delhi), 1960.

Siddiqui Asiya, *Agrarian change in the Northern Indian State* (*U.P. 1819-1933*) (Oxford Clarendon Press, New Delhi), 1973.

Singh Abhalakshmi, *Economics and geography of agricultural land reclamation* (B.R. Publishing Corporation, Vivekanand Nagar, Delhi), 1978.

Singh Jasbir, *An agricultural atlas of India : A geographical analysis* (Vishal Publications, Kurukshetra, Haryana) 1974.

Singh Jasbir, *An agricultural geography of Haryana* (Vishal Publications, Kurukshetra, Haryana), 1976.

Singh M, *Land utilization in Eastern Uttar Pradesh*, PhD thesis.

Singh NT, *Reclamation of alkali* (*kallar*) *soils* (Punjab Agricultural University, Ludhiana), 1972.

Singh RL, *India regional geography* (Varanasi), 1971.

Singh Shrinath, *Modernization of agriculture : A case study of Eastern Uttar Pradesh* (Heritage Publishers, New Delhi), 1976.

Spate OHK & Learmonth, ASJA, *India and Pakistan* (London), 1968.

Stamp LD, *Applied geography* (Penguin Books, London), 1960.

Stamp LD, *Our developing world* (London), 1960.

Stamp LD, *The land of Britain: Its use and misuse* (London), 1962.

Subramanian C, *The new strategy of Indian agriculture* (Vikas Publishing House, New Delhi), 1979.

Symons L, *Agricultural geography* (Bell's London), 1968.

Wadia DN, *Geology pf India* (London), 1960.

Yadav HR, *Wastelands diagnosis and treatment* (Concept Publishing Co., New Delhi), 1987.

Yadav HR, *Genesis and utilization of wastelands* (Concept Publishing Co, New Delhi), 1986.

(2) ARTICLES

Abrol IP & Bhumbla DR, paper presented at FAO/UNDP Seminar of Soil Survey and Soil Fertility Research, 15-20 February 1971, New Delhi, FAO, World Soil Research Rep. No 46.

Abrol IP, Reclamation of wastelands and world food prospects, *Trans Int. Cong Soil Sci, New Delhi,* 1982.

Abrol IP & Joshi PK, Economic viability of reclamation of alkali lands with special reference to agriculture and forestry. *Economics of wastelands development* (Society for Promotion of Wastelands Development, New Delhi), 1984.

Aggarwal VP, *background note on reclamation of alkali usar area of Uttar Pradesh,* in *Economics of wasteland development* (Society for Promotion of Wastelands Development, New Delhi), 1984.

Agarwal LT & Mehrotra CL, *Soil survey and soil work in U.P. Vol-I* (Allahabad), 1951.

Aggarwal LI, *Soil survey and soil work in U.P., Vol II* (Allahabad), 1952.

Aggarwal LI, *Soil survey and soil work in U.P., Vol III* (Allahabad), 1953.

Aggarwal LI, *Soil survey and soil work in U.P., Vol IV* (Allahabad), 1954.

Agharwal RR, Alkali soiis can be reclaimed, *Indian Fmg* **7** (9) (1957).

Agarwal RR, Potential and economic aspects of utilization of saline alkali soils, *Proc Seminar on Recent Advances in Agronomy and Soil Science*, Simla (Indian Council of Agricultural Research, New Delhi), 1959.

Agarwal RR & Gupta CP, Spread and intensity of soil alkalinity with canal irrigation in Gangetic alluvium of UP, *Indian J. agric Sci,* **27** (1957).

Agarwal RR & Gupta RN, Saline alkali soils in India, *I.C.A.R. Tech Bull* (*Agricultural Ser*), No 15, 1968.

Agarwal RR & Mehrotra CL, Quality of irrigation waters in UP, *Indian J Sci*, **31** (1966).

Agarwal RR & Yadav JSP, Saline and alkali soils of the Indian Gangetic alluvium in UP. *J Soil Sci*, **5** (2) (1954).

Agarwal RR, & Mehrotra CL, *Soil survey and soil, work in UP, Vol. I-IV* (Superintendant, Printing and Stationery UP, Allahabad), 1950-58.

Agarwal RR, Singh M & Pal C, *Daincha as a green manure in UP*, *Bull Dep Agric UP*, 1957.

Akachuku AE, *Cost-benefit analysis of wood and food components of agri-siliviculture in Nigerian forest zone*, *Agroforestry Systems*, 1985.

Ahmad, Enayat, Drainage and agriculture, in *Perspectives in Agricultural Geography*, Vol. II edited by N. Mohammad (New Delhi), 1980.

Anita Kumari & Kohli RK, Studies on dormancy and macromolecular drifts during germination in *Cassia occidentalis* L. *seeds*, *J Tree Sci*, **3** (1984),

Reclamation of Kans land India, *Ministry of Agriculture*, *Series I*, *Pamph No 2*. Delhi, 1949.

Arnold GW, *Ethology of Free Ranging Animals*, Division of Land Resource Management (SIRO, Wembley, SA, Australia), 1978.

Auden JA *et al.* Reports on sodium salts in reh soils in the United Provinces with notes on occurrences in other parts of India, *Rec geol Surv India*, 77 (1) (1942).

Blandford HF, Hotwinds of Northern India, *Mem Indian*, *met Dep*, Vol. 6, 1896.

Blandford HF, The rainfall of India, *Mem Indian met Dep*, Vol. 3, 1986-88.

Banerjee AK, Reclamation of wastelands in laterite tracts of Eastern India, *Mem Indian met Dep*, 43-122.

Barnes JH & Barkat Ali, Alkali soils, some biochemical factors in their reclamation, Report on Bihar ond Orissa, *Department of Agriculture of Agric India* (1930-31), 12.

Basu Subhashrajan, Physical factors affecting agriculture : A geographical analysis, in *Perspectives in agricultural geography*, Vol. II, by Noor Mohammad (Concept Publishing Co, New Delhi), 1977.

Bhumbla DR, Management of salt affected soils, in *Proc Indo-Hungrarin Seminar*, CSSRI, Karnal, 1977.

Bhumbla DR & Khare Arvind, Estimate of wastelands in India, in *Wastelands diagnosis and treatment* by HR Yadav (Concept Publising Co, New Delhi), 1987.

Bhumbla DR, Note on reclamation of alkali soils in uttar Pradesh, *Seminar-cum-workshop on Afforestation of Usar Wastelands* (Society for Promotion of Wasteland Development, New Delhi), 1985.

Bhudhyan Chattopadhyay & Moonis Raza, Regional development, *Indian J Reg Sci*, **8** (1) (1975).

Burrard SG, *On the origin of Himalayan Mountains, Geological Survey of India, Prof Paper No*. 12, 1942.

Chinnamani S, *Forestry, Social Forestry and Agroforestry in Ravine Reclamation*.

Chopra DP, *Promising Horticultural and Plants of Economic Importance for Wastelands*,

Chowdhry, Kamla, Greening of India, *Indian Express*. 21 December 1982.

Chowdhhury SG, Alkali soil, I, *Allahabad, Fmg* (1935), 9.

Chowdhhury SG, Alakli soil, II, *Allahabad Fmg* (1935), 9.

Chowdhhury SG, Alkali soils, III, *Allahabad Fmg* (1935) 9.

Ciriacy-Wantrup SV, Natural Resources in Economic Growth: The Role of Institutions and Policies, in *Perspectives in agricultural geography*, edited by N. Moha mmad (Concept Publishing Co, New Delhi), 1980.

Clark KGT, The Vicissitudes of the Summer Rainfall of the Indo-Gangetic Plain and the Valley, *Geography,* **18** (Pt IV) (1932).

Cowie NM, A criticism of Gldham's paper on the structure of Himalayas and of the Gangetic plain as elucidated by geodetic observations in India, *Mem geol Surv India, Professional Paper No. 18*, Dehradun, 1921.

DacGregor NM & Datta SK, The utilization of wastelands, *Indian Tea Ass Tocklai Exp. Sta. Mem No. 20*, Calcutta, 1947, 19.

Dei NK, Fertility and productivity of soil, in *Perspectives in agricultural geography*, Vol. 2, edited by N. Mohammad (Concept Publishing Co, New Delhi), 1980.

Dhir RP, Organisations involved or concerned in development of wasteland, in *Perspectives in agricultural geography*, edited by N. Mohammad (Concept Publishing Co, New Delhi), 1980.

Dhir RP, Concept and definition of wasteland, *Proc ICAR Sponsored Summer Institute* (Central Arid Zone Research Institute, Jodhpur), 1986.

Dhar NR, Mukherjee SK & Biswas NN, *Alkali soils and their reclamation*, *Current Reports* (Academy of Agriculture, New Delhi), 1938, 23.

Dhawan CL, *Land reclamation*, Central Board of Irrigation & *Power Publication No. 43*, Vol III, 1.

Eliot J, The hot winds of Northern India, *Indian met Mem*, **6** (Pt) (III), (1900).

Gedroiz KK, Saline soils and their improvement, *J exp Agron*, (in Russian: translated by SA Waksman).

Glennie EA, Gravity anomalies in the structure of the earth's crust, *Mem geol Surv India Prof Paper No. 27*, Dehradun, 1932.

Grandt AF & Lang AL, *Reclaiming Illinois stripwal land with legumes and grasses, Agric Exp. Sta Illinois Bull. No.* 628, Lerbana, 1958.

Hauser DP, Some problems in the use of stepwise regression technique in geographical research, ***Can Geogr***, **18** (1974), 1.

Hedge NG, ***Wasteland** development : Alternative to Prosopis juliflora.*

Hill EG, The analysis of reh, the alkaline salts in Indian usar land, *Chemical News* (1903), 87.

Hilgard EW, *Report of the Reh **Committee** for Investigating into the **causes** of the **Deterioration** of **Land** by Reh in **Aligarh District** in Alkali Lands, Irrigation and Drainage.* University of California, Appendix VII to Report for the year 1885: also *Dictionary of Economic Products, Vol. VI*, Part I, 1886.

Hill SA. Variations of rainfall in Northern India, ***Indian met Mem*, 1** (*Pt III*) 1897.

Hoon RC, *Land reclamation* (Central Board of Irrigation, India) **2** (43) 1955.

Hyden HH, Notes on the relationship of Himalaya to the Indo-Gangetic plain and the Indian peninsula, *Mem geol Surv India, Prof Paper No* 27, Dehradun, 1932.

Jana MM, Physical factors affecting agriculture in a backward region, in ***Perspectives in agricultural** geography*, Vol. 2, edited by Noor Mohammad (Concept Publishing Co, New Delhi) 1980.

Khanduri HC, *Reclamation of usar land for agriculture by afforestation*, in *Persvectives in agnicultural geography* (Concept Publishing Co, New Delhi) 1980.

Kamps LF, Mud distribution and land reclamation in Eastern Wadden Shallows, *Netherlands International Institute for Land Reclamation and Improvement Publication No*. 9, Wageningen, 1963.

Kanwar JS, Reclaiming deteriorated soils, *Fertil News*, **6** (21) (1961).

Kanwar JS, *Reclamation of saline alkali soils: quality of water required for leaching*, Paper presented at Symposium on Alkalinity and Salinity (Indian Agricultural Research Institute, New Delhi), 1962.

Kanwar JS, *Reclamation of saline, alkali soils, amendments, kinds amounts and costs*, Paper presented at Symposium on Salinity and Alkanity (Indian Agricultural Research Institute, New Delhi), 1962.

Kanwar JS & Bhumbla DR, Economic possibilities of utilising saline and alkali soils, *Proc Seminar on Recent Advances in Agronomy and Soil Science* (Indian Council of Agricultural Research, New Delhi), 1959.

Kar Amal, Land man and desert degradation : Geomorphic problems of agriculture in western Rajasthan, in *Perspectives in agricultural geography*, Vol 2, edited by N Mohammad (Concept Publishing Co., New Delhi) 1980.

Kar Anita & Kar Amal, Relevance of geomorphology in agricultural planning: Some global examples, in *Perspectives in agricultural geography*, Vol II, edited by N Mohammad (Concept Publishing Co, New Delhi) 1980.

Kaul KN, *Scheme for reclamation and development of usar lands, report, Indian Council of Agricultural Research Scheme, Delhi*, 1961.

Kennedy K, Australia's wasteland is now bountiful, *Indian Fmg*, **11** (10) (1962) 29.

Khan AD, *Usar soils, their indentification and reclamation*, Agriculture, Animal Husbundry, UP, 1950, 5.

Khan AD, It can certainly be done, *J Soil Wat Conserv in India*, **8** (1960).

Khan AD, *Diagnosis and reclamation of usar soils, Bureau of Agricultural Information, Tech Bull No* 4, Lucknow, 1951.

Leather JW, *Reclamation of usar resor land, Burean of Agricultural Information, Tech Ball No* 4, 1951, 7, 9, 13, 37.

Leather JW, Agricultural Soils, in *Agrl Ledger*, **3** (1898).

Leather JW, Reclamation of reh or usar soils, *Agrl Ledger*, (1893) 12, 13.

Mathur RK, Economics of agroforestry for wasteland reclamation, *Agrl Ledger*, (1893) 175-87.

Milne RA & Rapp E, *Salinity and drainge problems, causes, effects, managements, United States Department of Agriculture Farmers Bull No.* 1314. Washington, 1968.

Mishra Rajbans, Dayan SN & Bhola, *Economics of ravine afforestation with special reference to Chambal ravines*, Soil Conservation Research, Demonstration and Training Centre, Kota, 1967.

Mittal JP, *Role of livestock farming in wasteland development* (Soil Conservation Research Demonstration, Training Center, Kota) 1967.

Mustafa K, Tolba *Rolling Back the Wasteland*, Lecture delivered at a meet organized by the Society for Promotion of Wastelands Development, India International Centre, New Delhi, 27 December 1982.

Oldham RD, The structure of Himalayas and Gangetic plain, *Mem geol Surv India and Burma*, 3rd Edn, Vol I. Delhi, 1917.

Oldham RD, The deep boring at Lucknow, *Rec geol Surv India*, Vol. 23.

Pant SC, Role of NABARD in reclamation of wasteland, *Rec geol Surv India*, Vol. 23.

Parshad R & Yadav JSP, *Alkali soil reclamation questions and answers* (Central Soil Research Institute, Karnal).

Poscoe EH, *A manual of geology of India and Burwa*, 3rd Edn Vol. I, (Delhi) 1950.

Raheja RC *et al*, *Study of suitable trees, grasses and crops for saline and alkali land*, Working Group on Waste Land including Saline, Alkali and Waterlogged Lands, Government of India, 1962.

Raj SKT, *Ganga Khadir, A study on land reclamation in India, Ministry of Information and Broadcasting Pamph* No. 4, New Delhi, 1951, 44.

Raychaudhuri SP, Extensions of cultivated area for increased agricultural production, *Proc Symposium on Science and India's Food Problem* (ICAR, New Delhi) 1971.

Raychaudhury SP & Biswas NRD, Saline alkali soils of Asia with particular reference to India, *Trans 5th International Congress*, 1954.

Raychaudhuri SP, Final report of the All India Soil Survey Scheme, *Bull Indian Counc agric Res*, 1952, 13.

Sarkar Vinod, Vegetation of semi-arid wastelands and indicators of degradation.

Sen AK, Land utilization mapping to estimate the wasteland of arid zone by photo-interpretation technique, 49-53.

Sen AK, Typology of wastelands and mapping procedures in Rajasthan.

Saxena SK, Economic attributes of some multipurpose plants needed for wasteland Development.

Shah Parmesh, Economics of wasteland development projects undertaken by Gujarat State Rural Development Corporation, 189-213.

Shafi M, The problem of wastelands in India, in *The Geographer* (Sp. No.), **21** (1968), International Geographical Congress India, **15** (November 1968). Aligarh Muslim University Geographicel Society, Aligarh (India).

Shankarnarayan KA, Agroforestry, the key to rehabilitation of wasteland.

Shankar Narayan KA, Sen AK & Balakran, Analysis of wastelands in arid zone by remote sensing techniques, 55-64.

Sharma HS, Genesis of ravines of the Lower Chambal Valley, India, Selected papers, *Proc 21st International Geographical Union Congress*, **1** (1968) 114-18.

Sharma K, Prospects of integrating agroforestry with goal husbandry for economic upliftment or rural poor in wasteland of India.

Shrivastava KB, Role of prosopis in wastelands development.

Signond AA Joe, The alkali soils in Hungary and their reclamation measures, *Soil Sci*, **I8** (1924) 379-81.

Srivastava PBL, Mehrotra CL & Agarwal RR, The effect of leaching saline, alkali soil with irrigation waters of different kinds on the permeability and composition of the soils and the composition of leachets, *Jl India Soc Soil Sci*, (1962) 10.

Singh RP, Dryland agriculture and wasteland development.

Stamp LD, The land utilization survey of Britain, *Geograph J, Lond*, **78** (1931).

Subhashranjan Basu, Physical factors affecting agriculture : A geographical analysis, in, *Perspectives in agricultural geography*, edited by Noor Mohammad (Concept Publishing Co., New Delhi) 1980.

Venkataraman KG, Designing, planning and financing of tree plantation projects over state lands, in *Perspectives in agricultural geography*, edited by Noor Mohammad (Concept Publising Co, New Delhi) 1980, 221-25.

Verma Balvir : Principles and practices in gully reclamation.

Thomas KM & Srinivasan AS, Weed killers, *Indian Fmg*, **10**(2) (1949).

Taylor CC, Weed control, *Indian Fmg*, **9** (4) (1948).

Taylor CS, Effects of salt on soils, *Q J Dep Agric, Bengal* (1919).

Taylor EM, Making land reclamation profitable, *Indtan Fmg*, **1** (9) (1940).

Uppal HL, Reclaiming alkali wastelands, *ICAR Bull No* 85, New Delhi, 1961.

Uppal HL, *Reclamation of saline and alkali soils* (Land Reclamation, Irrigation and Power Research Institute, Punjab) 1962.

Uppal HL *et al. Reclamation of saline and alkaline lands, India* (Directorate of Extension Farm, No. 66, New Delhi), 1961.

Uppal HL, Agarwal RR & Kibe M, *Alkaline Lands Farm Bull No. 66*, Farming Information Unit Directorate of Extension, Ministry of Food and Agriculture, New Delhi, 1961.

Wadia DN & Auden JB, Geology structure of Northern India, *Mem geol Surv, India*, **78** (1939).

Whyte RD & Sisam JWC, *The establishment of vegetation on industrial wasteland, Common Agr. Bur. Joint* Publ No-14, 1949.

Yadav JSP, Usar soils, their characteristics and exploitation in forestry, *Proc. 9th Science Congress*, Part I, 1956.

Yadav JSP & Aggarwal RR, Dynamics of soil changes in the reclamation of saline alkali soils of the Indo-Gangetic alluvium, *Indian Soc Soil Sci*, (1979) 7.

Yadav JSP & Agarwal RR, A comparative study of effectiveness of gypsum and dhaincha in the reclamation of saline-alikali soils, *J Indian Soc Soil Sci*, (1961) 9.

(3) GOVERNMENT AND U.N. PUBLICATION

Academy of Sciences of the USSR, *The application of drainage in the reclamation of salinized soils*, translated from Russian, Moscow, 1958.

Agricultural Census of Uttar Pradesh, 1970-71 *Agricultural Statistics of Uttar Pradesh*, 1971.

Bulletin of Agricultural Statistics for Uttar Pradesh (1970-71) Joint Director for Statistics, Directorate of Agriculture, U.P. (India), 1972, 16.

Census of India, 1981, *Series I-India*, Part IIB(t). *Primary Census Abstract*. General Population Table, 1981.

Government of India, *Indian Agriculture in Brief*, Eighth Edition.

District Census Handbook, Sultanpur District, 1971, Series 21 UP, Part X-B, *Primary Census Abstract*, 1971.

F.A.O. A Framework for land evaluation, *Soil Bull* No. 1, 1976.

I.C.A.R. *Final Report of All India Soil Survey Scheme*, 1958.

I.C.A.R. *Handbook of Agriculture*, 1969.

Indian National Science Academy, *Proc Symposium on Reclamation and Use of Wastelands in India*, Bulletin No. 44, INSA, New Delhi, 1968.

Research and Reference Division, Ministry of Information and Broadcating, Government of India, *India 1972*: *A Reference Manual*, 1972, 250.

Ministry of Food and Agriculture, Government of India, Wasteland Survey and Reclamation Committee, *Report on the location and utilzation of wastelands in the* Part X. U.P. New Delhi, 1961.

National Botanic Gardens Lucknow, *Conquest of Usar (An experiment in reclamation of alkali land at Benthara, Lucknow District by biological and agronomic methods)*, 1961, 24.

Planning Commission, Programme Evaluation Organization, *Study of soil conservation programme for agricultural land*, New Delhi, 1964.

Planning Commission, Committee on Natural Resources, *Study of survey and reclamation of revines in India*, 1965.

Planning Commisson, Committee on Natural Resources, *Study on wastelands, including saline, alkali and water-logged lands and their reclamation measures*, New Delhi, 1963.

Proc natn Inst Sci India, **26** (*Suppl.*) (Pt A) : *Physical Sciences*, National Institute of Sciences of India, New Delhi, 1960.

Recommendations regarding the revision of the National Forest Policy, Department of Environment, Govt. of India, New Delhi.

State Soil Conservation Research *Annual Report, State Soil Conservation Research, U.P.*, 1961.

Statistical Book, District Sultanpur, Sultanpur, 1981-82.

Survey of India : *Topographical Sheets* No. 63 F/11, 63 F/10, 63 F/12, 63 F/14, 63 F/15, 63 F/16, 63 J/3, 63 J/4, 63 J/8, 63 J/11, 63/12, 63 K/5, 63 K/9.

The Times of India, Directory and Year Book including who's who, 1972, 192.

United Provinces of Agra and Oudh, Department of Agriculture 1909, *Reclamation of usar land, Report of Agra and Oudh.* Department of Agriculture, U.P., 1908-9.

Usar Land Reclamation Committee, U.P. *Report of usar land reclamation Committee*, (Superintendent, Printing and Stationery, Allahabad), 1938.

U.S.A. Salinity Lab *Diagnosis and improvement of saline and alkali soils Handbook*, U.S. Department of Agriculture No. 60, 1954.

U.S.D.A. *A manul on conservation of soil and water, Handbook of Professional Agricultural Workers* (Oxford Publishing Co) 1984.

The Imperial Gazetteer of India, Vol XXIII, Singhbhumi to Trashi-Chod-Zong, Reprint Edition (Today and Tomorrow Printers and Publishers, New Delhi) 1974, 130-37.

Wasteland Survey and Reclamation Committee, Ministry of Food anb Agriculture, *Report on location and utilisation of wasteland in India*, Part X, Uttar Pradesh, 1961.

Index